Trenching at Gallipoli

Trenching at Gallipoli

The Personal Narrative of a
Newfoundlander With the Ill-Fated
Dardanelles Expedition

John Gallishaw

LEONAUR

Trenching at Gallipoli: the Personal Narrative of a Newfoundlander
With the Ill-Fated Dardanelles Expedition
by John Gallishaw

Published by Leonaur Ltd

Material original to this edition and this editorial selection
copyright © 2011 Leonaur Ltd

ISBN: 978-0-85706-587-2 (hardcover)
ISBN: 978-0-85706-588-9 (softcover)

http://www.leonaur.com

Publisher's Notes

The views expressed in this book are not necessarily
those of the publisher.

Contents

To Professor Charles Townsend Copeland

Of all that Harvard has given me I value most
The friendship and confidence of "Copey"

The reader is hereby cautioned against regarding this narrative as in any way official. It is merely a record of the personal experiences of a member of the First Newfoundland Regiment, but the incidents described all actually occurred.

CHAPTER 1

Getting There

"Great Britain is at War."

The announcement came to Newfoundland out of a clear sky. Confirming it, came the news of the assurances of loyalty from the different colonies, expressed in terms of men and equipment. Newfoundland was not to be outdone. Her population is a little more than two hundred thousand, and her isolated position made garrisons unnecessary. Her only semblance of military training was her city brigades. People remembered that in the Boer War a handful of Newfoundlanders had enlisted in Canadian regiments, but never before had there been any talk of Newfoundland sending a contingent made up entirely of her own people and representing her as a colony. From the posting of the first notices bearing the simple message, "Your King and Country Need You," a motley crowd streamed into the armoury in St. John's. The city brigades, composed mostly of young, beautifully fit athletes from rowing crews, football and hockey teams, enlisted in a body. Every train from the interior brought lumbermen, fresh from the mills and forests, husky, steel-muscled, pugnacious at the most peaceful times, frankly spoiling for excitement. From the out-harbours and fishing villages came callous-handed fishermen, with backs a little bowed from straining at the oar, accustomed to a life of danger. Every day there came to the armoury loose-jointed, easy-swinging trappers and woodsmen, simple-spoken young men, who, in offering their keenness of vision and sureness of marksmanship, were volunteering their all.

It was ideal material for soldiers. In two days many more than the required quota had presented themselves. Only five hundred men could be prepared in time to cross with the first contingent of Canadians. Over a thousand men offered. A corps of doctors asked impertinent questions concerning men's ancestors, inspected teeth, measured and pounded chests, demanded gymnastic stunts, and finally sorted out the best for the first contingent. The disappointed ones were consoled by news of another contingent to follow in six weeks. Some men, turned down for minor defects, immediately went to hospital, were treated, and enlisted in the next contingent.

Seven weeks after the outbreak of war the Newfoundlanders joined the flotilla containing the first contingent of Canadians. Escorted by cruisers and air scouts they crossed the Atlantic safely and went under canvas in the mud and wet of Salisbury Plain, in October, 1914. To the men from the interior, rain and exposure were nothing new. Hunting deer in the woods and birds in the marshes means just such conditions. The others soon became hardened to it. They had about settled down when they were sent on garrison duty, first to Fort George in the north of Scotland, and then to Edinburgh Castle. Ten months of bayonet-fighting, physical drill, and twenty-mile route marches over Scottish hills moulded them into trim, erect, bronzed soldiers.

In July of 1915, while the Newfoundlanders were under canvas at Stob's Camp, about fifty miles from Edinburgh, I was transferred to London to keep the records of the regiment for the War Office. At any other time I should have welcomed the appointment. But then it looked like quitting. The battalion had just received orders to move to Aldershot. While we were garrisoning Edinburgh Castle, word came of the landing of the Australians and New Zealanders at Gallipoli. At Ypres, the Canadians had just then recaptured their guns and made for themselves a deathless name. The Newfoundlanders felt that as colonials they had been overlooked. They were not militaristic, and they hated the ordinary routine of army life, but they wanted to do their share. That was the spirit all through the regiment. It was the spirit that possessed them on the long-waited-for day at Aldershot when Kitchener himself pronounced them "just the men I want for the Dardanelles."

That day at Aldershot every man was given a chance to go back to Newfoundland. They had enlisted for one year only, and any man that wished to could demand to be sent home at the end of the year; and when Kitchener reviewed them, ten months of that year had gone. With the chance to go home in his grasp, every man of the first battalion reenlisted for the duration of the war. And it is on record to their eternal honour, that during the week preceding their departure from Aldershot, breaches of discipline were unknown; for over their heads hung the fear that they would be punished by being kept back from active service. To break a rule that week carried with it the suspicion of cowardice. This was the more remarkable, because many of the men were fishermen, trappers, hunters, and lumbermen, who, until their enlistment had said "Sir" to no man, and who gloried in the reputation given them by one inspecting officer as "the most undisciplined lot he had ever seen." From the day the Canadians left Salisbury Plain for the trenches of Flanders, the Newfoundlanders had been obsessed by one idea: they must get to the front.

I was in London when I heard of the inspection at Aldershot by Lord Kitchener, and of its results. I had expected to be able to rejoin my battalion in time to go with them to the Dardanelles; but when I applied for a transfer, I was told that I should have to stay in London. I tried to imagine myself explaining it to my friends in No. 11 section who were soon to embark for the Mediterranean. Apart altogether from that, I had gone through nearly a year of training, had slept on the ground in wet clothes, had drilled from early morning till late afternoon, and was perfectly fit. It had been pretty strenuous training, and I did not want to waste it in an office.

That evening I applied to the captain in charge of the office for a pass to Aldershot to bid good-by to my friends in the regiment. He granted it; and the next morning a train whirled me through pleasant English country to Aldershot. At the station I met an English Tommy.

"I suppose you're looking for the Newfoundlanders," he said, glancing at my shoulder badges. I was still wearing the service uniform I had worn in camp in Scotland, for I had not been regularly attached to the office force in London.

"I'll take you to Wellington Barracks," volunteered the Englishman. "That's where your lot is."

We trudged through sand, on to a gravel road, through the main street of the town of Aldershot, and into an asphalt square,

Lord Kitchener talking to some Australians at Anzac

surrounded by brick buildings, three storied, with iron-railed verandas. Men in khaki leaned over the veranda rails, smoking and talking. A regiment was just swinging in through one of the gaps between the lines.

"Company, at the halt, facing left, form close column of platoons." Company B of the First Newfoundland Regiment swung into position and halted in the square just in front of their quarters. "Company, Dismiss!" Hands smacked smartly on rifle stocks, heels clicked together, and the men of B Company fell out. A gray-haired, iron-moustached soldier, indelibly stamped English regular, carrying a bucket of swill across the square to the dump, stopped to watch them.

"Wonder who the new lot is?" said he to a comrade lounging near. "I cawn't place their bloomin' badge."

"'Aven't you 'eard?" said the other. "Blawsted colonials; Canydians, I reckon."

A tall, loose-jointed, sandy-haired youth who approached the two was unmistakably a colonial; there was a certain ranginess that no amount of drilling could ever entirely eradicate.

"Hello, Poppa," he greeted the gray-haired one, who had now resumed his journey toward the dump. "What will you answer when your children say, 'Daddy, what part did you play in the great war?'"

He of the swill bucket spat contemptuously, disdaining to answer. The sandy-haired youth continued airily across the square and up the stairs that led to his quarters. I followed him up the stairs and through a door on which was printed "Thirty-two men," and below, in chalk, "B Company." We entered a long, bare-looking room, down each side of which ran rows of iron cots. Equipments were piled neatly on the beds and on shelves above; two iron-legged, barrack-room tables and a few benches completed the furniture. At one of the tables sat two young men. One of them, a massively built young giant, looked up as the door opened.

"Hello, Art," he said to my conductor. "You're just the man we want. Don't you want to join us in a party to go up to London?"

"No," answered Art; "if you break leave this week, you don't get to the front."

The big fellow stretched his massive frame in a capacious yawn.

"I don't think we'll ever get to the front," he said. "This isn't a

15

regiment. It's an officers' training corps. They gave out a lot more stripes to-day, and one fellow got a star—made him a second lieutenant. You'd think this was the American army; it's nothing but stars and stripes. Soon 't will be an honour to be a private. The worst of it is, they'll come along to me and say, 'What's your name and number?' The only time they ever talk to me is to ask me my name and number; and when I tell them, they put me on crime for not calling them 'Sir,' and when I don't they have me up for insolence."

Art laughed. "Cheer up, old boy," he said; "you'll soon be at the front, and then you won't have to call anybody 'Sir.'"

"What's the latest news about the regiment?" I inquired of my conductor.

"I suppose you know that the king and Lord Kitchener reviewed us," he said, "and this afternoon we are to be reviewed once more. It's a formality. We should leave this evening or to-morrow for the front. I suppose we'll go to some seaport town and embark there."

While we were talking a bugle blew. "There's the cook-house bugle," said Art. "Come along and have some dinner with us." He took some tin dishes from the shelves above the beds, gave me one, and we joined in the rush down the stairs and across the square to the cook house.

In the army, the cook house corresponds to the dining-room of civilization. B Company cook house was a long, narrow, wooden building. On each side of a middle aisle that led to the kitchen were plain wooden tables, each accommodating sixteen men, eight on each side. When we arrived, the building was full. When you are eating as the guest of the Government, there is no hostess to reserve for you the choice portions; therefore it behoves you to come early. In the army, if you are not there at the beginning of a meal, you go hungry. Thus are inculcated habits of punctuality. But if you are called and the meal is not ready, you have your revenge. Two hundred and sixty-two men of B Company were showing their disapproval of the cooks' lack of punctuality. Screeches, yells, and cat cries rivalled the din of stamping feet and the banging of tin dishes. Occasionally the door of the kitchen swung open and afforded a glimpse of three sweating cooks and their group of helpers, working frenziedly. Sometimes the noise stopped long enough to allow some spokesman to express his opinion of the cooks, and their fitness for their jobs, with that delightful simplicity and charming candour that made the language of the First Newfoundland Regiment so refreshing. Loud applause served the double purpose of encouraging the speakers and drowning the reply of the incensed cooks. This was a pity, because the language of an army cook is worth hearing, and very enlightening. Men who formerly prided themselves on their profanity have listened, envious and subdued, awed by the originality and scope of a cook's vocabulary, and thenceforth quit, realizing their own amateurishness. Occasionally, though, one of the cooks, stung to retort, would appear, wiping his hands on his overalls, and in a few well-chosen phrases, cover some of the more recent exploits of the one who had angered him, or endeavour to clear his own character, always in language brilliant, fluent, and descriptive.

But the longest wait must come to an end, and at last the door of the kitchen swung open and the helpers appeared. Some mysterious mess fund had been tapped, and that day dinner was particularly good. First came soup, then a liberal helping of roast beef, with potatoes, tomatoes, and peas, followed by plum pudding. B Company soon finished. In the army, dinner is a thing not of ceremony, but of necessity.

I did not wait for my sandy-haired friend; his name, I gathered, was Art Pratt. He and a neighbour were adjusting a difference regarding the ownership of a combination knife, fork, and spoon. I found my way back to the room marked "Thirty-two men." Just as I entered, I heard the bugle sound the "half-hour dress."

All about the room men were busy shining shoes, polishing buttons, rolling puttees, and adjusting equipments. This took time, and the half hour for preparation soon passed. In the square below, at the sound of the "Fall In," eleven hundred men of the first battalion of the First Newfoundland Regiment sprang briskly to attention. After their commanding officer had inspected them, the battalion formed into column of route. As the tail of the column swung through the square, I joined in. A short march along the Aldershot Road brought us to the dusty parade ground. Here we were drawn up in review order, to await the inspecting general. When he arrived, he rode quickly through the lines, then ordered the men to be formed into a three-sided square. From the centre of this human stadium he addressed them.

"Men of the First Newfoundland Regiment," said he, "a week ago you were reviewed by His Majesty the King and by Lord Kitchener. On that day, Lord Kitchener told you that you were just the men he needed for the Dardanelles. I have been deputed to tell you that you are to embark to-night. You have come many miles to help us; and when you reach the Dardanelles, you will be opposed by the bravest fighters in the world. It is my duty and my pleasure on behalf of the British Government and of His Majesty the King to thank you and to wish you God-speed."

This was the moment the Newfoundlanders had been waiting for for nearly a year. From eleven hundred throats broke forth wave upon wave of cheering. Then came an instant's hush, the bugle band played the general salute, and the regiment presented arms. Gravely the general acknowledged the compliment, spurred his horse, and rode rapidly away. The regiment reformed, marched back to barracks, and dismissed.

I joined the crowd that pressed around the board on which were posted the daily orders. My friend Art Pratt was acting as spokesman.

"A and B Companies leave here at eight this evening," he said. "C and D Companies an hour later. They march to Aldershot railway station, and entrain there."

I left the group around the board and walked over to the office of the adjutant. He was busy giving instructions about his baggage.

"Well," he said, "what do you want?"

"I want to go with the battalion this evening, sir," I said.

He questioned me; and when he found out all the facts, told me that I couldn't go. I didn't wait any longer. As I went out the door, I could just hear him murmur something about my not having the necessary papers. But I wasn't thinking of papers just then. I was wondering how I could get away. I vowed that if I could possibly do it I would go with the battalion. I was passing one of the stairways when I heard some one yell, "Is that you, Corporal Gallishaw?" I turned. It was Sam Hiscock, one of my old section.

"Hello, Sam," I said. "I didn't know where to look for old No. 11 section. They've all been changed about since they came here."

"Come up this way," said Sam, and I followed him up the stairs and into a room occupied by the men of No. 11 section, my old section at Stob's Camp in Scotland.

Disconsolately I told them my plight, and disclosed my plan guardedly. Sam Hiscock, faithful and loyal to his section, voiced the sentiment. "Come on with old No. 11; we'll look after you. All you have to do is hang around here, and when we're moving off just fall in with us, and nobody'll notice then; 't will be dark."

"The big trouble is," I said, "I have no equipment, no overcoat, no kit-bag; in fact, no anything."

"You've got a rain coat," said Pierce Power, "and I've got a belt you can have." Another offered a piece of shoulder strap, and some one else volunteered to show me where a pile of equipments were kept in a room. I followed him out to the room. In the corner a man was sitting on the floor, smoking. He was the guard over the equipments. He belonged to an English regiment, and so did the equipments. Sam Hiscock engaged him in conversation for a few minutes. The topic he introduced was a timely one: beer. While Hiscock and the guard went to the canteen to do some research work in beverages, I took his place guarding the equipments. By the time the two returned I had managed to acquire a passable looking kit. I spent the rest of the afternoon going around among my friends and telling them what I proposed to do. At eight o'clock I joined the crowd that cheered A and B Companies as they moved away, in charge of the adjutant and the colonel. When the major called C and D Companies to attention, I fell in with my old section C Company. The lieutenant in charge of the platoon I was with saw me, but in the dusk he could not recognize my face. I was thankful for the convenient darkness; and because it was fear of his invention that caused it, I blessed the name of Count Zeppelin.

"Where's your rifle?" asked the lieutenant.

"Haven't got one, sir," I said.

The lieutenant called the platoon sergeant. "Sergeant," he snapped, "get that man a rifle." The sergeant doubled back to the barracks and returned with a rifle. The lieutenant moved away, and I had just begun to congratulate myself, when disaster overtook me. The platoon was numbered off. There was one man too many, and of course I was the man. The lieutenant did not waste any time in vain controversy. He ordered me out of his platoon.

"Where shall I go?" I asked.

"As far as I am concerned," he answered, "you can go straight to hell."

I left his platoon; but when I did, I carried with me the precious rifle. The sergeant, a thorough man, had been thoughtful enough to bring with it a bayonet.

The time had now come to risk everything on one throw. I did. In the army, all orders from the commanding officer of a regiment are transmitted through the adjutant. I knew that both the colonel and the adjutant had gone an hour ago, and could not now be reached. So I walked up to Captain March, the captain of D Company, saluted, and told him that I had been ordered to join his company.

"Ordered by whom?" he asked.

"By the adjutant," said I, brazenly.

"I haven't had any orders about that," said Captain March.

Just then, Captain O'Brien, who had been my company commander in camp, came up. I think he must have known what I was trying to do.

"If the adjutant said so, it's all right," he said, thus leaving the burden of proof on me.

"Go ahead then," said Captain March; "fall in."

I fell in. We formed up, and swung out of the square and along the road that led to the station. At intervals, where a street lamp threw a subdued glare, crowds cheered us; for even Aldershot, clearing house of fighting forces, had not yet ceased to thrill at the sight of men leaving for the front. Half an hour after we left the barracks, we were all safely stowed away in the train, ten men in each of the compartment coaches. Just as we were pulling out, a soldier went from coach to coach, shaking hands with all the men. He came to our coach, put his head in through the window, and shook hands with each man. I was on the inside. "Good-by, old chap," he said, then gasped in astonishment. The train was just beginning to move. It was well under way when he recovered himself. "Gallishaw," he shouted, "you're under arrest." It was the sergeant-major of the Record Office I had quitted in London.

During war time in England, troop trains have the right of way over all others. All night our train rattled along, with only one stop. That was at Exeter where we were given a lunch supplied by the mayoress and ladies of the town. I spent the night under the seat; for I thought the sergeant-major might telegraph to have the train searched for me. Early next morning, we shunted onto a wharf in Devonport, alongside the converted cruiser *Megantic*. Her sides were already lined with soldiers; another battalion of eleven hundred men, the Warwickshire Regiment, was aboard. As soon as our battalion had detrained, I hid behind some boxes on the pier; and when the last of the men were walking up the gangplank. I joined them. A steward handed each man a ticket, bearing the number of his berth. I received one with the rest. Since I was in uniform, the steward had no way of telling whether or not I belonged to the Newfoundlanders.

All that day the *Megantic* stayed in port, waiting for darkness to begin the voyage. In the afternoon, we pulled out into the stream; and at sunset began threading our way between buoys, down the tortuous channel to the open sea. A couple of wicked-looking destroyers escorted us out of Devonport; but as soon as we had cleared the harbour, they steamed up and shot ahead of us. The next morning they had disappeared. The first night out I ate nothing, but the next day I managed to secure a ticket to the dining-room. With two battalions on board, there was no room on the *Megantic* for drills; the only work we had was boat drill once a day. Each man was assigned his place in the lifeboats. At the stern of the ship a big 4.7 gun was mounted; and at various other points were placed five or six machine guns, in preparation for a possible submarine attack. In addition, we depended for escape on our speed of twenty-three to twenty-five knots.

During the boat drills, I stayed below with the Warwickshire Regiment, or, as we called them, the Warwicks. This regiment was formed of men of the regular army, who had been all through the first gruelling part of the campaign, beginning with the retreat from Mons, to the battle of the Marne. They were the remnants of "French's contemptible little army." Every one of them had been wounded so seriously as to be unable to return to the front. Ordinarily they would have been discharged, but they were men whose

21

whole lives had been spent in the army. Few of them were under forty, so they were now being sent to Khartoum in the Sudan, for garrison duty. At night, I came on deck. In the submarine area ships showed no lights, so I could go around without fear of discovery. The only people I had to avoid were the officers, and the caste system of the army kept them to their own part of the ship. The men I knew would sooner cut their tongues out than inform on me.

Just before sunset of the third night out, because we passed several ships, we knew we were approaching land. At nine o'clock, we were directly opposite the Rock of Gibraltar. After we had left Gibraltar behind, all precautions were doubled; we were now in the zone of submarine operations. Ordinarily we steamed along at eighteen or nineteen knots; but the night before we fetched Malta, we zigzagged through the darkness, with engines throbbing at top speed, until the entire ship quivered and shook, and every bolt groaned in protest. With nearly three thousand lives in his care, our captain ran no risks. But the night passed without incident. The next day, at noon, we were safe in one of the fortified harbours of Malta.

After we left Malta, since I knew I could not then be sent back to England, I reported myself to the adjutant. He and the colonel were in the orderly room, as the office of a regiment is called. The sergeant-major in charge of the orderly room had been taken ill two or three days before, and the other men had been swamped by the extra rush of clerical work, incident on the departure of a regiment for the front. Perhaps this had a good deal to do with the lenient treatment I received. The adjutant came to the point at once. That is a characteristic of adjutants.

"Gallishaw," he said, "do you want to come to work here?"

"Yes, sir," I answered.

"All right," he said; "you're posted to B Company."

That night, it appeared in orders that "Lance-Corporal Gallishaw has embarked with the battalion, and is posted to B Company for pay." The only comment the colonel made on the affair was to say to the adjutant, "I've often heard of men leaving a ship when she is going on active service, but I've never heard of men stowing away to get there." Thus I went to work in the orderly room; and in the orderly room I stayed until we arrived at Alexandria, Egypt, and

Scene at Lancashire Landing, Cape Helles

entrained for Cairo. At Heliopolis, on the desert near Cairo, we went into camp. There I joined my company and drilled with it, and bade good-by to the orderly room and all its works.

We stayed in Egypt only ten days or so to get accustomed to the heat, and to change our heavy uniforms and hats for the light-weight duck uniforms and sun helmets, suitable for the climate on the Peninsula of Gallipoli. The heat at Heliopolis was too intense to permit of our drilling very much. In the very early morning, before the sun was really strong, we marched out a mile across the desert, skirmished about for an hour or so, and returned to camp for breakfast. The rest of the day we were free. Ordinarily we spent the morning sweltering in our marquees, saying unprintable and uncomplimentary things about the Egyptian weather. In the late afternoon and evening, we went to Cairo. About a mile from where we were camped, a street car line ran into the city. To get to it we generally rode across the desert on donkeys. Every afternoon, as soon as we had finished dinner, little native boys pestered us to hire donkeys. They were the same boys who poked their heads into our marquees each morning and implored us to buy papers. We needed no reveille in Egypt. The thing that woke us was a native yelling "Eengaleesh paper, veera good; veera good, veera nice; fifty thousand Eengaleesh killed in the Dardanelle; veera good, veera nice."

About a quarter of a mile across the desert from us was a camp for convalescent Australians and New Zealanders. As soon as the Australians found that we were colonials like themselves, they opened their hearts to us in the breezy way that is characteristically Australian. There is a Canadian hospital unit in Cairo. One medical school from Ontario enlisted almost *en masse*. Professors and pupils carry on work and lectures in Egypt just as they did in Canada. It was not an uncommon thing to see on a Cairo street a group composed of an Australian, a New Zealander, a Canadian, and a Newfoundlander. And once we managed to rake up a South African. The clean-cut, alert-looking, bronzed Australians, who impressed you as having been raised far from cities, made a tremendous hit with the Newfoundlanders. One chap who was returning home minus a leg, gave us a young wallaby that he had brought with him from Australia. One of our boys had a small donkey, not much larger than a collie dog, that he bought from a native for a few shillings. The men vied with each other in feeding the animals. Some fellows took the kangaroo one evening, and he acquired a taste for beer. The donkey's taste for the same beverage was already well developed. After that, the two were the centre of convivial gatherings. The wallaby got drunk faster, but the donkey generally got away with more beer. When we were certain we were to go to the front, a meeting was held in our marquee. It was unanimously decided that not a man was to take a cent with him—everybody was to leave for the front absolutely broke—"to avoid litigation among our heirs," the spokesman said. The wallaby and the donkey benefited. The night before we left the desert camp, they were wined and dined. The next morning, the kangaroo, bearing unmistakable marks of his debauch, showed up to say good-by. We were not allowed to take him with us, and he was relegated to the Zoo in Cairo. The donkey, who had been steadily mixing his drinks from four o'clock the afternoon before, did not see us go. When we moved off, he was lying unconscious under one of the transport wagons.

Although we took advantage of every opportunity for pleasure, we had not lost sight of our real object. We were grateful for a chance to visit the Pyramids, and enjoyed our meeting with the men from the Antipodes, but Egypt soon palled. The Newfoundlanders' comment was always the same. "It's some place, but it isn't the front. We came to fight, not for sightseeing."

CHAPTER 2

There

It was with eleven hundred eager spirits that I lined up on a Sunday evening early in August, 1915, on the deck of a troopship, in Mudros Harbour, which is the centre of the historic island of Lemnos, about fifty miles from Gallipoli. Around us lay all sorts of ships, from ocean leviathans to tiny launches and rowboats. There were gray and black-painted troopers, their rails lined with soldiers, immense four-funnelled men-o'-war, and brightly lighted, white hospital ships, with their red crosses outlined in electric lights. The landing officer left us in a little motor boat. We watched him glide slowly shoreward, where we could faintly discern through the dusk the white of the tents that were the headquarters for the army at Lemnos. To the right of the tents, we could see the hospital for wounded Australians and New Zealanders. A French battleship dipped its flag as it passed, and our boys sang the Marseillaise.

A mail that had come that day was being sorted. While we waited, each man was served with his "iron ration." This consisted of a one-pound tin of pressed corn beef—the much-hated and much-maligned "bully beef"—a bag of biscuits, and a small tin that held two tubes of "Oxo," with tea and sugar in specially constructed air-and-damp-proof envelopes. This was an emergency ration, to be kept in case of direst need, and to be used only to ward off actual starvation. After that, we were given our ammunition, two hundred and fifty rounds to each man.

But what brought home to me most the seriousness of our venture was the solitary sheet of letter paper with its envelope, that was given to every man, to be used for a parting letter home. For some poor chaps it was indeed the last letter. Then we went over the side, and aboard the destroyer that was to take us to Suvla Bay.

The night had been well chosen for a surprise landing. There was no moon, but after a little while the stars came out. Away on the port bow we could see the dusky outline of land; and once, when we were about half way, an airship soared phantom-like out of the night, poised over us a short time, then ducked out of sight. At first the word ran along the line that it was a hostile airship, but a few inquiries soon reassured us.

Suddenly we changed our direction. We were near Cape Hellas, which is the lowest point of the Peninsula of Gallipoli. Under Sir Ian Hamilton's scheme, it was here that a decoy party was to land to draw the Turks from Anzac. Simultaneously, an overwhelming force was to land at Suvla Bay and at Anzac, to make a surprise attack on the Turks' right flank. Presently, we were going up shore past the wrecked steamer *River Clyde*, the famous "Ship of Troy," from the side of which the Australians had issued after the ship had been beached; past the shore hitherto nameless, but now known as Anzac. Australian, New Zealand, Army Corps, those five letters stand for; but to those of us who have been on Gallipoli, they stand for a great deal more: they represent the achievement of the impossible. They are a glorious record of sacrifice, reckless devotion, and unselfish courage. To put each letter there cost the men from Australasia ten thousand of their best soldiers.

And so we edged our way along, fearing mines, or, even more disastrous than mines, discovery by the enemy. From the Australians over at Anzac, we could hear desultory rifle fire. Once we heard the boom of some big guns that seemed almost alongside the ship. Four hours it took us to go fifty miles, in a destroyer that could make thirty-two knots easily. By one o'clock, the stars had disappeared, and for perhaps three quarters of an hour we edged our way through pitch darkness. We gradually slowed down, until we had almost stopped. Something scraped along our side. Somebody said it was a floating mine, but it turned out to be a buoy that had been put there by the navy to mark the channel. Out of the gloom directly in front some one hailed, and our people answered.

"Who have you on board?" we heard the casual English voice say. Then came the reply from our colonel:

"Newfoundlanders."

There was to me something reassuring about that cool, self-contained voice out of the night. It made me feel that we were being expected and looked after.

"Move up those boats," I heard the English voice say, and from right under our bow a naval launch, with a middy in charge, swerved alongside. In a little while it, with its string of boats, was securely fastened.

Just before we went into the boats, the adjutant passed me.

"Well," he said, "you've got your wish. In a few minutes you'll be ashore. Let me know how you like it when you're there a little while."

"Yes, sir," I said. But I never had a chance to tell him. The first shrapnel shell fired at the Newfoundlanders burst near him, and he had scarcely landed when he was taken off the Peninsula, seriously wounded.

In a short time we had all filed into the boats. There was no noise, no excitement; just now and then a whispered command. I was in a tug with about twenty others who formed the rear guard. The wind had freshened considerably, and was now blowing so hard that our unwieldy tug dared not risk a landing. We came in near enough to watch the other boats. About twenty yards from shore they grounded. We could see the boys jump over the side and wade ashore. Through the half darkness we could barely distinguish them forming up on the beach. Soon they were lost to sight.

During the Turkish summer, dawn comes early. We transhipped from our tug to a lighter. When it grounded on the beach, day was just breaking. Daylight disclosed a steeply sloping beach, scarred with ravines. The place where we landed ran between sheer cliffs. A short distance up the hill we could see our battalion digging themselves in. To the left I could see the boats of another battalion. Even as I watched, the enemy's artillery located them. It was the first shell I had ever heard. It came over the hill close to me, screeching through the air like an express train going over a bridge at night. Just over the boat I was watching it exploded. A few of the soldiers slipped quietly from their seats to the bottom of the boat. At first I did not realize that anybody had been hit. There was no sign of anything having happened out of the ordinary, no confusion. As

Allies landing reinforcements under heavy fire of Turks in Dardanelles

soon as the boat touched the beach, the wounded men were carried by their mates up the hill to a temporary dressing station. The first shell was the beginning of a bombardment. "Beachy Bill," a battery that we were to become better acquainted with, was in excellent shape. Every few minutes a shell burst close to us. Shrapnel bullets and fragments of shell casing forced us to huddle under the baggage for protection. A little to the left, some Australians were severely punished. Shell after shell burst among them. A regiment of Sikh troops, mule drivers, and transport men were caught half way up the beach. Above the din of falling shrapnel and the shriek of flying shells rose the piercing scream of wounded mules. The Newfoundlanders did not escape. That morning "Beachy Bill's" gunners played no favourites. On all sides the shrapnel came in a shower. Less often a cloud of thick black smoke, and a hole twenty feet deep showed the landing place of a high explosive shell. The most amazing thing was the coolness of the men. The Newfoundlanders might have been practising trench digging in camp in Scotland. When a man was hit, some one gave him first aid, directed the stretcher bearers where to find him, and resumed digging.

About nine, I was told off to go to the beach with one man to guard the baggage. We picked our way carefully, taking advantage of every bit of cover. About half way down, we heard the warning shriek of a shell, and threw ourselves on our faces. Almost instantly we were in the centre of a perfect whirlwind of shells. "Beachy Bill" had just located a lot of Australians, digging themselves in about fifty yards away from us. The first few shells fell short, but only the first few. After that, the Turkish gunners got the range, and the Australians had to move, followed by the shells. As soon as we were sure that the danger was over, we continued to the beach, and aboard the lighter that contained our baggage. We had not had a chance to get any breakfast before we started, but the sergeant of our platoon had promised to send a corporal and another man to relieve us in two hours. About twelve o'clock the sergeant appeared, to tell me to wait until one o'clock, when I should be relieved. He brought the news that the adjutant had been wounded seriously in the arm and leg. At the very beginning of the bombardment, a shell had hit him. About forty of our men had been hit, the sergeant said, and the regiment was preparing to change its position. He showed us the new position, and told us to rejoin there as soon as relieved.

About a hundred yards to the right of us rose a cliff that prevented our boat being seen by the enemy. The Turks were devoting their attention to some boats landing well to the left of us. The officer in charge of landing was taking advantage of this and had a gang near us working on dugouts for stores and supplies. Right under the cliffs a detachment of engineers were building a landing as coolly as if they were at home. Every fifteen or twenty minutes, to show us that he was still doing business, "Beachy Bill" sent over a few shells in our direction. The gunners could not see us, but they wanted to warn us not to presume too much. As soon as the first shell landed near us, the officer in charge shouted nonchalantly, "Take cover, everybody." He waited until he was certain every man had found a hiding place, then effaced himself. The courage of the officers of the English army amounts almost to foolhardiness. The men to relieve us did not arrive at once, as promised. The hot afternoon passed slowly. Each hour was a repetition of the preceding one. "Beachy Bill" was surpassing himself. From far out in the bay our warships replied.

About five o'clock I espied one of the Newfoundland lieutenants a little way up the beach in charge of a party of twenty men. I signalled to him and he came down to our boat. The party had come to unload the baggage. When I asked the lieutenant about being relieved, he told me that he had sent a corporal and one man down about one o'clock, and ordered me back to the regiment to report to Lieutenant Steele. Half way up the beach we found Lieutenant Steele. The corporal sent down to relieve me, he told me, had been hit by a shell just after he left his dugout. The man with him had not been heard from. I went back to the beach, and found the man perched up on top of the cliff to the right of the lighter. He had been waiting there all the afternoon for the corporal to join him.

Having solved the mystery of the failure of the relief party, I returned to my platoon. Their first stopping place had proved untenable. All day they had been subjected to a merciless and devastating shelling, and their first day of war had cost them sixty-five men. They were now dug in in a new and safer position. They were only waiting for darkness to advance to reinforce the firing line that was now about four miles ahead. Since to get to our firing line we had to cross the dried-up bed of a salt lake, no move could be made in daylight. That evening we received our ration of rum, and formed up silently in a long line two deep, beside our dugouts. I fell in with my section, beside Art Pratt, the sandy-haired chap I had met in Aldershot. He had been cleaning his rifle that afternoon when a shell landed right in his dugout, wounded the man next him, knocked the bolt of the rifle out of his hand, but left him unhurt. He accepted it as an omen that he would come out all right, and was grinning delightedly while he confided to me his narrow escape, and was as happy as a school-boy at the thought of getting into action.

Under cover of darkness we moved away silently, until we came to the border of the Salt Lake. Here we extended, and crossed it in open order, then through three miles of knee high, prickly un-derbrush, to where our division was entrenched. Our orders were to reinforce the Irish. The Irish sadly needed reinforcing. Some of them had been on the Peninsula for months. Many of them are still there. From the beach to the firing line is not over four miles, but it is a ghastly four miles of graveyard. Everywhere along the route are small wooden crosses, mute record of advances. Where the crosses are thickest, there the fighting was fiercest; and where the fight-ing was fiercest, there were the Irish. On every cross, besides a man's name and the date of his death, is the name of his regiment. No other regiments have so many crosses as the Dublins and the Munsters. And where the shrapnel flew so fast that bodies mangled beyond hope of identity were buried in a common grave, there also are the Dublins and the Munsters; and the cross over them reads, "In Memory of Unknown Comrades."

The line on the left was held by the Twenty-ninth Division; the Dublins, the Munsters, the King's Own Scottish Borderers, and the Newfoundlanders made up the Eighty-eighth Brigade. The Newfoundlanders were reinforcements. From the very first day of the Gallipoli campaign, the other three regiments had formed part of what General Sir Ian Hamilton in his report calls "The incomparable Twenty-ninth Division." When the first land-ing was made, this division, with the New Zealanders, penetrated to the top of Achi Baba, the hill that commanded the Narrows.

Troops at the Dardanelles leaving for the landing beach

For forty-eight hours the result was in doubt. The British attacked with bayonet and bombs, were driven back, and repeatedly re-attacked. The New Zealanders finally succeeded in reaching the top, followed by the Eighty-eighth Brigade. The Irish fought on the tracks of a railroad that leads into Constantinople. At the end of forty-eight hours of attacks and counter attacks, the position was considered secure. The worn-out soldiers were relieved and went into dugouts. Then the relieving troops were attacked by an overwhelming hostile force, and the hill was lost. A battery placed on that hill could have shelled the Narrows and opened to our ships the way to Constantinople. The hill was never retaken. When reinforcements came up it was too late. The reinforcements lost their way. In his report, General Hamilton attributes our defeat to "fatal inertia." Just how fatal was that inertia was known only to those who formed some of the burial parties.

After the first forty-eight hours we settled down to regular trench warfare. The routine was four days in the trenches, eight days in rest dugouts, four days in the trenches again, and so forth, although three or four months later our ranks were so depleted that we stayed in eight days and rested only four. We had expected four days' rest after our first trip to the firing line, but at the end of two days came word of a determined advance of the enemy. We arrived just in time to beat it off. Our trenches instead of being at the top were at the foot of the hill that meant so much to us.

The ground here was a series of four or five hog-back ridges, about a hundred yards apart. Behind these towered the hill that was our objective. From the nearest ridge, about seven hundred yards in front of us, the Turks had all that day constantly issued in mass formation. During that attack we were repaid for the havoc wrought by Beachy Bill. As soon as the Turks topped the crest, they were subjected to a demoralizing rain of shell from the navy and from our artillery. Against the hazy blue of the skyline we could see the dark mass clearly silhouetted. Every few seconds, when a shell landed in the middle of the approaching columns, the sides of the column would bulge outward for an instant, then close in again. Meanwhile, every man in our trenches stood on the firing platform, head and shoulders above the parapet, with fixed bayonet and loaded rifle, waiting for the order to begin firing. Still the

Turks came on, big, black, bewhiskered six footers, reforming ranks and filling up their gaps with fresh men. Now they were only six hundred yards away. But still there was no order to open fire. It was uncanny. At five hundred yards our fire was still withheld. When the order came, "At four hundred yards, rapid fire," everybody was tingling with excitement. Still the Turks came on, magnificently determined, but it was too desperate a venture. The chances against them were too great, our artillery and machine gun fire too destructively accurate. Some few Turks reached almost to our trenches, only to be stopped by rifle bullets. "Allah! Allah!" yelled the Turks, as they came on. A sweating, grimly happy machine gun sergeant was shouting to the Turkish army in general, "It's not a damn bit of good to yell to Allah now." Our artillery opened huge gaps in their lines, our machine guns piled them dead in the ranks where they stood. Our own casualties were very slight; but of the waves of Turks that surged over the crest all that day, only a mere shattered remnant ever straggled back to their own lines.

That was the last big attack the Turks made. From that time on, it was virtually two armies in a state of siege. That was the first night the Newfoundlanders went into the trenches as a unit. A and B Companies held the firing line, C and D were in the support trenches. Before that, they filled up gaps in the Dublins or in the Munsters, or in the King's Own Scottish Borderers. These regiments were our tutors. Mostly they were composed of veterans who had put in years of training in Egypt or in India. The Irish were jolly, laughing men with a soft brogue, and an amazing sense of humour. The Scotch were dour, silent men, who wasted few words. Some of the Scotchmen were young fellows who had been recruited in Scotland after war broke out. One of these chaps shared my watch with me the first night. At dark, sentry groups were formed, three reliefs of two men each; these two men stood with their heads over the parapet watching for any movement in the no man's land between the lines; that accounts for the surprisingly large number of men one sees wounded in the head. The Scottie and I stood close enough together to carry on a conversation in whispers. It turned out that he had been training in Scotland at the same camp where the Newfoundlanders were. He had been on the Peninsula since April, and was all in from dysentery and lack of food. "Nae meat," was the laconic way he expressed it. Like every Scotchman since the world began, he answered to the name of "Mac." He pointed out to me the position of the enemy trenches.

"It's just aboot fower hundred yairds," he said, "but you'll no get a chance to fire; there's wurrkin' pairties oot the nicht." Then as an afterthought, he added gloomily, "There's no chance of your gettin' hit either."

"Why," I asked him in astonishment, "you don't want to get hit, do you?"

Mac looking at me pityingly. "Man," he burst out, "when ye're here as long as I've been here, ye'll be prayin' fer a 'Blighty one.'"

Blighty is the Tommies' nickname for London, and a "Blighty one" is a wound that's serious enough to cause your return to London.

For a few minutes Mac continued looking over the parapet. Without turning his head, he said to me: "I'll gie ye five poond, if ye'll shoot me through the airm or the fut." When a Scotchman who is getting only a shilling a day offers you five pounds, it is for something very desirable. Before I had a chance to take him up on this handsome offer, my attention was attracted by the appearance of a light just a little in front of where Mac had said the enemy trench was located. I grabbed my gun excitedly.

"Dinna fire, lad," cautioned Mac. "We have a wurrkin' pairty oot just in front. Ye would na hit anything if ye did. 'Tis only wastin' bullets to fire at night."

For almost an hour I continued to watch the light as it moved about. It was a party of Turks, Mac explained, seeking their dead for burial. When I was relieved for a couple of hours' sleep they were still there.

Just where I was posted, the trench was traversed; that is, from the parapet there ran at right angles, for about six feet, a barricade of sandbags, that formed the upright line of a figure T. The angle made by this traverse gave some protection from the wind that swept through the trench. Here I spread my blanket. The night was bitterly cold, and I shivered for lack of an overcoat. In coming away hurriedly from London, I did not take an overcoat with me. In Egypt, it had never occurred to me that I should need one in Gallipoli; and the chance to get one I had lost. But I was too weary to let even the cold keep me awake. In a few minutes I was as sound asleep as if I had been far from all thought of war or trenches.

It seemed to me that I had just got to sleep when I was awakened by a hand shaking my shoulder roughly, and by a voice shouting, "Stand to, laddie." It was Mac. I jumped to my feet, rubbing my eyes.

"What's the matter?" I asked.

"Nothing's the matter," said Mac. "Every morning at daybreak ye stand to airms for an hour."

I looked along the trench. Every man stood on the firing platform with his bayonet fixed. Daybreak and just about sunset are the times attacks are most likely to take place. At those times the greatest precautions are taken. Dawn was just purpling the range of hills directly in front when word came, "Day duties commence." Periscopes were served out, and placed about ten feet apart along the trench. These are plain oblong tubes of tin, three by six inches, about two feet high. They contain an arrangement of double mirrors, one at the top, and one at the bottom. The top mirror slants backward, and reflects objects in front of it. The one at the bottom slants forward, and reflects the image caught by the top mirror. In the daytime, by using a periscope, a sentry can keep his head below the top of the parapet, while he watches the ground in front. Sometimes, however, a bullet strikes one of the mirrors, and the splintered glass blinds the sentry. It is not an uncommon thing to see a man go to the hospital with his face badly lacerated by periscope glass.

During the daytime, the men who were not watching worked at different "fatigues." Parapets had to be fixed up, trenches deepened, drains and dumps dug, and bomb-proof shelters had to be constructed for the officers. Every few minutes the Turkish batteries opened fire on us, but with very poor success. The navy and our land batteries replied, with what effect we could not tell. Once or twice I put my head up higher than the parapet. Each time I did, I heard the ping of a bullet, as it whizzed past my ear. Once a sniper put five at me in rapid succession. Every one was within a few inches of me, but fortunately on the outside of the parapet. Just before landing in Egypt, we had been served out with large white helmets to protect us from the sun. It did not take us very long to discover that on the Peninsula of Gallipoli these were veritable death traps. Against the landscape they loomed as large as tents; they were simply invitations to the enemy snipers. We soon discarded them for our service caps. The hot sun of a Turkish summer bored down on us, adding to the torment of parched throats and tongues. We were suffering very much from lack of water. The first night we went into the firing line we were issued about a pint of water for each man. It was a week before we got a fresh supply. We had not yet had time to get properly organized, and our only food was hard biscuits, apricot jam, and bully beef; a pretty good ration under ordinary conditions, but, without water, most unpalatable. The flies, too, bothered us incessantly. As soon as a man spread some jam on his biscuits, the flies swarmed upon it, and before he could get it to his mouth it was black with the pests.

These were not the only drawbacks. Directly in front of our trenches lay a lot of corpses, Turks who had been killed in the last attack. In front of the line of about two hundred yards held by B Company there were six or seven hundred of them. We could not get out to bury them, nor could we afford to allow the enemy to do so. There they stayed, and some of the hordes of flies that continually hovered about them, with every change of wind, swept down into our trenches, carrying to our food the germs of dysentery, enteric, and all the foul diseases that threaten men in the tropics.

After two days of this life, we were relieved and moved back about two miles to the reserve dugouts for a rest, to get something to eat, and depopulate our underwear; for the trenches where we slept harboured not only rats but vermin and all manner of things foul.

The regiment that relieved us was an English regiment, the Essex. They were some of "Kitchener's Army." We stood down off the parapet, and the Englishmen took our places. Then with our entire equipment on our backs we started our hegira. We had about four miles to go, two down through the front line trenches, then two more through winding, narrow communication trenches, almost to the edge of the Salt Lake. Here in the partial shelter afforded by a small hill were our dugouts. In Gallipoli there was no attempt at the ambitious dugout one hears of on the Western front. Our dugouts resembled more nearly than anything else newly made graves. Usually one sought a large rock and made a dugout at the foot of

A REMARKABLE VIEW OF A LANDING PARTY IN THE DARDANELLES

it. The soil of the Peninsula lent itself readily to dugout construction. It is a moist, spongy clay, of the consistency of thick mortar. A pickaxe turns up large chunks of it; these are placed around the sides. A few hours' sun dries out the moisture, and leaves them as hard and solid as concrete.

While we had been in the firing line, another regiment had made some dugouts. There were four rows of them, one for each company. B Company's were nearest the beach. We filed slowly down the line, until we came to the end. A dugout was assigned to every two men. I shared one with a chap named Stenlake. We spread our blankets, put our packs under our heads, and for the first time for a week, took off our boots. Before going to sleep, Stenlake and I chatted for a while. When war broke out, he told me, he had been a missionary in Newfoundland. He offered as chaplain, and was accepted and given a commission as captain. Later some difficulty arose. The regiment was made up of three or four different denominations, about equally divided. Each one wanted its own chaplain, which was expensive; so they decided to have no chaplain. Stenlake immediately resigned his commission, and enlisted as a private.

Our whisperings were interrupted by a voice from the next dugout. "You had better get to sleep as soon as you can, boys; you have a hard day before you, to-morrow." It was Mr. Nunns, the lieutenant in command of our platoon. Casting aside all caste prejudice, he was sleeping in the midst of his men, in the first dugout he had found empty. He could have detailed some men to build him an elaborate dugout, but he preferred to be with his "boys." The English officers of the old school claim that this sort of thing hurts discipline. If they had seen the prompt and cheerful way in which No. 8 platoon obeyed Mr. Nunns' orders, they would have been enlightened.

CHAPTER 3

Trenches

Somebody has said that a change of occupation is a rest. Whoever sent us into dugouts for a rest, evidently had this definition in mind. After breakfast the first morning we were ordered out for digging fatigue just behind the firing line. In this there was one consolation. We did not have to carry our packs. Each man took his rifle and either a pick or a shovel. Communication trenches had to be dug to avoid long tramps through the firing line; and connecting trenches had to be made between the existing communication trenches. While we were in dugouts we had eight hours of this work out of every twenty-four; four hours in the daytime and four at night.

The second day in dugouts when we came back from our morning's digging, we found some new arrivals making some dugouts about two hundred yards behind our lines. They were Territorials, who correspond to the militia in the United States. "The London Terriers," they called themselves. Mostly they were young fellows from eighteen to twenty-two years old. They had landed only that morning and were in splendid condition, and very eager for the coming of evening when they were to go to the firing line. The ground they had selected was sheltered from observation by the little ridge near our line of dugouts; but some of our men in moving about attracted the attention of the Turkish artillery observer. Instantly half a dozen shells came over the ridge, past our line, and *bang!* right in the midst of the Londons, working fearful destruction. Every ten or fifteen minutes after that, the Turks sent over some shells. Some regiments are lucky, others seem to walk into destruction everywhere they turn. The shells fired at the Newfoundlanders landed in the Londons. About two minutes' walk from our dugouts our cooks had built a fire and were preparing meals. A number of our men passed continually between our line and the cooks'. Not one of them was even scratched. The only two of the Londons who ventured there were hit; one fellow was killed instantly, the other, seriously wounded through the lungs, lay moaning where he had fallen. It was just dusk, and nobody knew he had been hit until one of our men, coming down, heard his hoarse whispering request to "get a doctor, for God's sake get a doctor." While somebody ran for the doctor, our stretcher bearers responded to the all too familiar shout, "Stretcher bearers at the double," but by the time they reached him he was beyond all need of doctor or stretcher bearers. Before the London Terriers even saw the firing line, they lost over two hundred men. They simply could not escape the Turkish shells. The enemy had a habit of sending over one shell, then waiting just a minute or less, and following it with another. The first shell generally wounded two or three men; the second one was sent over to catch the stretcher bearers and the comrades who hastened to aid those who were hit. Before they had completed their dugouts, the shrapnel caught them in the open; after they were dug in, it buried them alive. Never did a regiment leave dugouts with so much joy as did the London Terriers when they entered the trenches for the first time. Ordinarily a man is much safer in the firing line than in rest dugouts. Trenches are so constructed that even when a shell drops right in the traverse where men are, only half a dozen or so suffer. In open or slightly protected ground where the dugouts are, the burst of a shrapnel shell covers an area twenty-five by two hundred yards in extent.

A shell can be heard coming. Experts claim to identify the calibre of a gun by the sound the shell makes. Few live long enough to become such experts. In Gallipoli the average length of life was three weeks. In dugouts we always ate our meals, such as they were, to the accompaniment of "Turkish Delight," the Newfoundlanders' name for shrapnel. We had become accustomed to rifle bullets. When you hear the zing of a spent bullet or the sharp crack of an explosive, you know it has passed you. The one that hits you, you never hear. At first we dodged at the sound of a passing bullet, but soon we came actually to believe

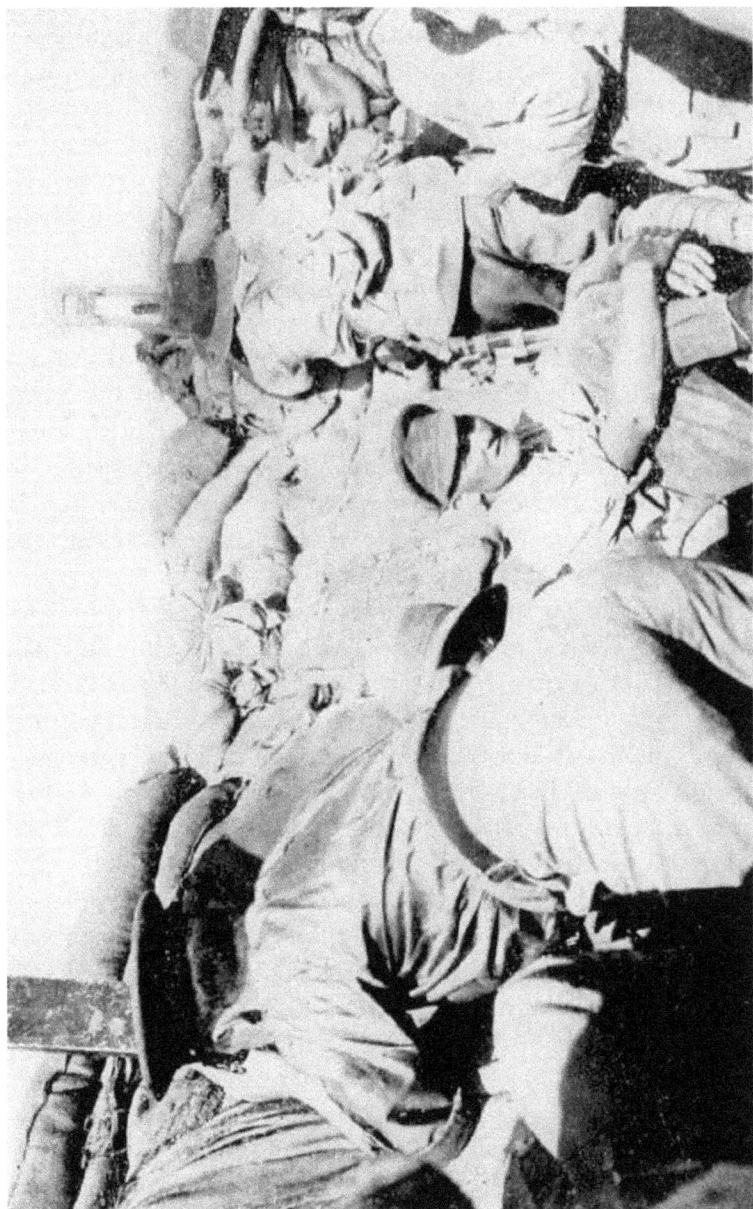

AUSTRALIANS IN TRENCH ON GALLIPOLI PENINSULA, USING THE PERISCOPE NOTE THE DIFFERENT SHAPED HATS WORN BY THE MEN, FIVE KINDS APPEARING IN THE LITTLE GROUP

the superstition that a bullet would not hit a man unless it had on it his regimental number and his name. Then, too, a bullet leaves a clean wound, and a man hit by it drops out quietly. The shrapnel makes nasty, jagged, hideous wounds, the horrible recollection of which lingers for days in the minds of those who see them. It is little wonder that we preferred the firing line.

Every afternoon from just behind our line of dugouts an aeroplane buzzed up. At the tremendous height it looked like an immense blue-bottle fly. We always knew when it was two o'clock. Promptly at that hour every afternoon it winged its way over us and beyond to the Turkish trenches. At first the enemy's aeroplanes came out to meet ours, but a few encounters with our men soon convinced them of the futility of such attempts. After that, they relied on their artillery. In the air all around the tiny speck we could see white puffs of smoke that showed where their shrapnel was exploding. Sometimes those puffs were perilously close to it; at such times our hearts were in our mouths. Everybody in the trench craned his neck to see. When our aeroplane manoeuvred clear, you could hear a sigh of relief from every man.

After about the eighth day in dugouts we were ordered back to the firing line. We had to take over a part of the trench near Anafarta village. In this vicinity the Fifth Norfolks, a company formed of men from the King's estate at Sandringham, had charged into the woods, about two hundred and fifty strong, and had been completely lost sight of. This was the most comfortable trench we had yet been in. It had been taken over from the Turks, and when we faced toward them we had to build another firing platform. This left their firing platform for us to sleep on. After the cramped, narrow trenches of the first couple of weeks, this roomy trench was very pleasant. On both sides of the trench were some trees that threw a grateful shade in the daytime. Along the edge grew little bushes that bore luscious blackberries, but to attempt to get them was courting death. Nevertheless, the Newfoundlanders secured a good many. Best of all though was the "Block House Well." For the first time we had a plenitude of water. But by this time conditions had begun to tell on the men. Each morning more and more men reported for sick parade. They were beginning to feel the enervating effect of the climate, and of the lack of water and proper food. While we were entrenched near the block house, the men were sickening so fast that in our platoon we had not enough men to form the sentry groups. The non-commissioned officers had to take their place on the parapet, and the ordinary work of the non-coms, changing sentries, waking reliefs, and detailing working parties had to be done by the commissioned officers. Just about an hour before my turn to watch, I was suddenly stricken by the fever that lurks on the Peninsula. In the army, no man is sick unless so pronounced by the medical officer. Each morning at nine there is a sick parade. A man taken ill after that has to wait until the next morning, and is officially fit for duty. My turn came at eleven o'clock at night. The man I was to relieve was Frank Lind. He went on at nine. When eleven o'clock came, I was burning up with fever. Lind would not hear of my being roused to relieve him, but continued on the parapet until one o'clock, although in that part of the trench snipers had been doing a lot of execution. Then he rested for a couple of hours and at three o'clock resumed his place on the parapet for the remainder of the night. At daybreak he was still there. I slept all through the night, exhausted by the fever, and it was not till a few days after that some one else told me what Lind had done. From him I heard no mention of it. Whenever somebody says that war serves only to bring out the worst in a man I think of Frank Lind. The fever that had weakened me so, continued all that day. I reported for sick parade and was given a day off duty. The next day I was given light duty, and the following day the fever left me and that night I was fit for duty again, and was sent out to a detached post about halfway between us and the enemy. The detached post was an abandoned house about twenty feet square. All the doors and windows had been torn out, and now it was nothing but the merest skeleton of a house. We had been there about three hours when there occurred something most extraordinary and unaccountable. It was a pitch dark night, and working parties were out from both sides. Ordinarily there would have been no firing. Suddenly from away on the right where the Australians were, began the sharp crackling of rapid fire. A boy pulling a wooden stick along an iron park railing makes almost the same sound. The crackling swept down the line right past the trench directly behind us and away on to the left. The Turks, fearing an attack, replied. Between the two fires we were caught. There were eight of us in the blockhouse. Only two of us came from No. 8 platoon, Art Pratt, my sandy-haired friend of Aldershot days, and I. The sergeant in charge was from another platoon. When the rapid fire began, he became melodramatic. He had the responsibility of seven other men's lives, and the thing that seemed rather comic to us was probably very serious to him. There was nothing the matter, though, with the way in which he handled the situation. There were eight openings in the house for the missing doors and windows. At each window he placed a man, and stood at the door himself, then ordered us to fill our magazines and fix our bayonets. But psychologically he made a mistake. He turned to me and said,

"Corporal, we're in a pretty tight place. We may have to sell our lives dearly. I want every man to stand by me. Will you stand by me?"

When the thing had started I had just experienced a pleasant tingle of excitement, but at this view of the situation I felt a little serious. Before I had a chance to reply Art Pratt relieved the situation by shouting,

"Did you say stand by you? I'll stand by this window and I'll bayonet the first damn Turk I see."

There was a general laugh and the moment of tension passed. In a few minutes the exchange of rapid fire died down as suddenly as it had started. The rest of the night passed uneventfully. Just before daybreak we returned to our platoons.

We never found out the reason for the sudden exchange of rapid fire. Some Australians away on the right had started it. Everybody had joined in, as the firing ran along the line of trenches. As soon as the officers began an investigation it was stopped.

It seems to me that most of the time we were in the blockhouse trench we spent our nights out between the lines. Most of our work was done at night. When we wished to advance our line, we sent forward a platoon of men the desired distance. Every man carried with him three empty sandbags and his entrenching tool. Temporary protection is secured at short notice by having every man dig a hole in the ground that is large and deep enough to allow him to lie flat in it. The entrenching tool is a miniature pickaxe, one end of which resembles a large bladed hoe with a sharpened and tempered edge. The pick end is used to loosen hard material and to break up large lumps; the other end is used as a shovel to throw up the dirt. When used in this fashion the wooden handle is laid aside, the pick end becomes a handle, and the entrenching tool is used in the same manner as a trowel. The whole instrument is not over a foot long, and is carried in the equipment.

Lying on our stomachs, our rifles close at hand, we dug furiously. First we loosened up enough earth in front of our heads to fill a sandbag. This sandbag we placed beside our heads on the side nearest the enemy. Out in no man's land with bullets from rifle and machine guns pattering about us, we did fast work. As soon as we had filled the second and third sandbags we placed them on top of the first. In Gallipoli every other military necessity was subordinated to concealment. Often we could complete a trench and occupy it before the enemy knew of it. In the daytime our aeroplanes kept their aerial observers from coming out to find any work we had done during the night. Sometimes while we were digging, the Turks surprised us by sending up star shells. They burst like rockets high overhead. Everything was outlined in a strange, uncanny light that gave the effect of stage fire. At first, when a man saw a star shell, he dropped flat on his face; but after a good many men had been riddled by bullets, we saw our mistake. The sudden, blinding glare makes it impossible to identify objects before the light fades. Star shells show only movement. The first stir between the lines becomes the target for both sides. So, after that, even when a man was standing upright, he simply stood still.

After the block-house trench, our next move was to a part of the firing line that I have never been able to identify. It was very close to the Turks, and in this spot we lost a large number of men. From one point, a narrow sap or rough trench ran out at right angles very close to the Turkish position. It may have been twenty-five or thirty yards away. To hold this sap was very important; if the Turks took it, it gave them a commanding position. About twenty men were in it all the time, four or five of them bomb throwers. The men holding this sap at the time we were there were the Irish, the Dublin Fusiliers or, as we knew them, the Dubs. The Turks made several attempts to take it, but were repulsed. When our men were not on sentry duty, several of them spent their rest hours out

First line of Allies' trench zigzagging along parallel to the Turkish trenches which are not thirty yards distant in this sap, talking to the Dubs. The Dubs were interesting talkers. They had been in the thing from the beginning, and spoke of the landings with laughter and a fierce joy of slaughter. Most of them had been on the Western front before coming to Gallipoli. From the Turkish trenches directly in front of this sap, the enemy signalled the effect of our shots. They used the same signals that we used in target practice, waving a stick back and forth to indicate outers, inners, magpies, and bull's-eyes. Whoever did it, had a sense of humour; because as soon as he became tired, he took down the stick for an instant, then raised it again and waved it back and forth derisively, with a large red German sausage on the end of it. This did not seem to bear out very well the tales that the enemy was slowly starving to death. Prisoners who surrendered from time to time told us that at any moment the entire Turkish army might surrender, as they were very short of food. One thing we did know: the Turks felt the lack of shoes; out between the lines we found numbers of our dead with the boots cut off.

While we were in this place the Turks dug to within ten or twelve yards of us before they were discovered. One of the Dublins saw them first. He seized some bombs, and jumped out, shouting, "Look at Johnny Turk. Let's bomb him to hell out of it." But Johnny Turk was obstinate; he stayed where he was in spite of our bombs. One of our fellows, the big chap whom I had heard at Aldershot complaining about being asked for his name and number, had crawled into the sap. He made his way through the smoke and dirt to the end of the sap where only a few yards separated him from the Turks. In one item of armament the British beat the Turks. We use bombs that explode three seconds after they are thrown; the Turks' don't explode for five seconds. The difference of only two seconds seems slight, but that day in the sap-head it was of great importance. For a short while the supply of bombs for our side ran out. The man who was trying to get the cover off a box of them found difficulty in doing it. The men in the sap-head were without bombs. Meanwhile the Turks kept up an uninterrupted throwing of bombs. Most of them landed in the sap. The big Newfoundlander who had crawled out looking for excitement found it. As soon as the supply of bombs ran out, instead of getting back into safety, he stood his ground. The first bomb that came over dropped close to him. He was swearing softly, and his face was glowing with pleasure. He bent down coolly, picked up the bomb and threw it back over the parapet at the Turks who had sent it. With our bombs he could not have done it, but the extra two seconds were just enough. Five or six of the bombs came in and were treated in the same way, before our supply was resumed. A brigade officer, who had come out into the sap, stood gazing awe-struck at the big Newfoundlander. Open-mouthed, with monocle in hand, the officer was the picture of amazement. At last he spoke, with that slow, impersonal English drawl:

"I say, my man, what is your name and number."

The look on the Newfoundlander's face was a study. He knew he should not have come out into that sap, and every time that question had been shot at him before it had meant a reprimand. At last he shrugged his shoulders, then with a resigned expression, answered the officer in a fashion not entirely confined to Newfoundlanders—by asking a question: "What in hell have I done now?"

Without a word the officer turned on his heel and left the sap. The big fellow waited until he felt the officer was well out of sight, then departed for his proper place in the trench. One of the Dubs looking after him, said to me:

"There's a man that would have been recommended for a Distinguished Conduct Medal if he'd answered that officer right."

That Irishman was a man of wide experience.

"I've been seventeen years in the army, and I've been in every war that England fought in that time," said he, "and I'll tell you now, the real Distinguished Conduct Medal men and the real V.C. heroes never get them. They're under the ground." Coming from the man it did, this expression of opinion was interesting, for he was Cooke, the man who had been given a Distinguished Conduct Medal for his work on the Western front. Since coming to the Peninsula he had been acting as a sharpshooter, and had been recommended for the V.C., the Victoria Cross, which is the highest reward for valour in the British army. He was only waiting then, for word to go to London, to get the cross pinned on by the King.

"There's one man on this Peninsula," continued Cooke, "who's won the V.C. fifty times over; that's the donkey-man."

The man Cooke meant was an Australian, a stretcher-bearer. His real name was Simpson, but nobody ever called him that. Because he was of Irish descent, the Australians, who dearly love nicknames, called him Murphy, or, Moriarty, or Dooley, or whatever Irish name first occurred to them. More generally, though, he was called the Man with the Donkey, and by this name he was known all over the Peninsula. In the early days, the Anzacs had captured some booty from the Turks and in it were some donkeys. It was in the strenuous time when men lay in all sorts of inaccessible places, dying and sorely wounded, Simpson in those days seemed everywhere. As soon as he heard of the capture he went down, looked appraisingly over the donkeys, and commandeered two of them. On one donkey he painted F.A. No. 1, and on the other, F.A. No. 2; F.A. being his abbreviation for Field Ambulance. Day and night after that Simpson could be seen going about among the wounded, here giving a man first aid, there loosening the equipment and making easier the last few minutes for some poor fellow too far gone to need any medical care. The wounded men who could not walk or limp down to the dressing station he carried down, one on each of the donkeys and one on his back or in his arms. He talked to the donkeys as they plodded slowly along, in a strange mixture of English, Arabic profanity, and Australian slang. Many an Australian or New Zealander who has never heard of Simpson remembers gratefully the attentions of a strangely gentle man who drove before him two small gray donkeys each of which carried a wounded soldier. In Australia long after this war is over men will thrill at the mention of the Man with the Donkey. I agreed with Cooke that this man had won the V.C. fifty times over.

Cooke was going out that night, he told me, to stay for three or four days, sniping, between the lines. As soon as he came back he expected to go to London.

"Before I go out," he said, "I'll show you a good place where you can get a shot at Abdul Pasha."

I followed Cooke out through the sap and up the trench a little way to where it turned sharply to avoid a large boulder. Just in front of this boulder was some short, prickly underbrush. Cooke parted the bushes cautiously with his hand, and motioned me to come closer. I did and through the opening he pointed out the enemy trench about four hundred yards away, and about thirty yards in front of it a little clump of bushes.

"Just in front of those bushes," said Cooke, "there's a sniper's dugout. Keep your eyes open to-morrow and you ought to get some of them."

I noted the place for the next day, and walked down to the sap with Cooke. There I shook hands with him, wished him good luck, and returned to my platoon.

That night I had to go out on listening patrol between the lines. At one o'clock my turn came. An Irish sergeant came along the trench for me to guide me out to the listening post. I went with him a short distance along the trench, picked up four others, then with a shoulder from a comrade, we got over the parapet. The listening post was about a hundred yards away. We had gone only a few yards when we heard firing coming from that direction, first one shot followed by twenty or thirty in quick succession, then silence. A man stumbled out of the darkness immediately in front of us. He was panting and excited. It was a messenger from the corporal that we were going to relieve. He had been walking along without the least suspicion of danger when he had run full tilt into a party of fifteen or sixteen of the enemy. He had dropped down immediately and yelled to one of his men to go back to the trench with word. We followed the panting messenger to the post. The enemy had now disappeared. We opened rapid fire in the direction in which they had gone. Evidently it was right, for in a few seconds they returned it, wounding one man. For about five minutes we kept up firing, with what success we could not tell, but at any rate we had the satisfaction of driving off a superior force. Those two hours straining through the darkness were not particularly pleasant. I did not know what moment or from what direction the enemy might come, and I knew that if he did come it would be in force. Apparently the whole thing was unplanned, because during the remainder of my two hours, although I peered unceasingly in all directions, I could see nothing, nor could I hear the slightest sound. Evidently Johnny Turk was willing to let well enough alone. That night when I returned to the trench I was told that the next night at dark we were to go into dugouts.

Ordinarily the thought of dugouts was distasteful, but it seemed years since I had taken my boots off. Our platoon had lost heavily, mostly from disease. All the novelty had worn off the trench life. Instead of six non-coms, there were only three. Each of us was doing the work of two men. Our ration had been the eternal bully beef, biscuit, and jam. Our cooks did their best to make it palatable by cooking the beef in stew with some desiccated vegetables, but these were hard and tasteless. Most of us had got to the stage where the very sight of jam made us sick. That night, looking down through the ravine, I saw, winking and blinking cheerfully, the only light that brightened the Stygian darkness, the Red Cross of the hospital ships. I have wondered since if the entrance to heaven is illuminated with an electric Red Cross. There was not a man in the whole battalion who was really fit. Most of them had had a touch of one or more of the prevalent diseases.

Stenlake, the young clergyman, who had been my dugout mate, was scarcely able to drag himself about the trench. And by this time we had the weather to contend with. It was nearing the middle of October, and the rainy season was almost upon us. Occasionally the sky darkened up to a heavy greyness that seemed to cover everything as with a pall. Following this came heavy, sudden squalls that swept through the trenches, drenching everything, and tearing blankets and equipments with them. Although the sun still continued to bore down unremittingly in the daytime, the nights had become bitterly cold, and to the tropical diseases were added rheumatism and pneumonia. On the men from Newfoundland the climate was especially telling. We had ceased to wonder at the crowd of men who reported sick each morning, and simply marvelled that the number was not greater.

All over the Peninsula disease had become epidemic until the clearing stations and the beaches were choked with sick. The time we should have been sleeping was spent in digging, but still the men worked uncomplainingly. Some, too game to quit, would not report to the doctor, working on courageously until they dropped, although down in the bay beckoned the Red Cross of the hospital ship, with its assurance of cleanliness, rest, and safety. By sickness and snipers' bullets we were losing thirty men a day. Nobody in the front line trenches or on the shell-swept area behind ever expected to leave the Peninsula alive. Their one hope was to get off wounded. Every night men leaving the trenches to bring up rations from the beach shook hands with their comrades. From every ration party of twenty men we always counted on losing two. Those who were wounded were looked on as lucky. The best thing we could wish a man was a "cushy wound," one that would not prove fatal, or a "Blighty one." But no one wanted to quit. Men hung on till the last minute. Often it was not till a man dropped exhausted that we learned from his comrades that he had not eaten for days. The only men in my platoon who seemed to be nearly fit were Art Pratt, and a young chap named Hayes. Art seemed to be enjoying the life thoroughly. He went about the trench, cheerfully, grinning and whistling, putting heart into the others. Whenever there was any specially dangerous work to be done, Art always volunteered. He spent more time out between the lines than in the trench. Whenever a specially reliable, cool man was needed, Art was selected. Young Hayes was a small chap who had been in my platoon at Stob's Camp in Scotland. He had made a record for being absent from parade, and was always in trouble for minor offenses. I took him in hand and did my best to keep him out of trouble. Out in the trenches he remembered it, and followed me around like a shadow. Whenever I was sent in charge of a fatigue party he always volunteered. The men all did their best to make the work of the non-coms easy. As a study in the effects of colonial discipline it would have been enlightening for some of the English officers. The men called their corporals and sergeants, Jack, or Bill, or Mac, but there never was the slightest question about obeying an order. Everybody knew that everybody else was overworked and underfed, and every man tried to give as little trouble as possible. Such conduct from the Newfoundlanders was astonishing, as in training they simply loved to make trouble for the non-coms, and the most unenviable job in the regiment was that of corporal or sergeant.

Such were the conditions the next afternoon when we moved from the firing trench to rest near some dugouts that had been forsaken by the Royal Scots. They had been relieved, some said, to go to the island of Imbros, about fifteen miles away, for a rest. At Imbros, rumour said, you could buy, in the canteen, eggs and butter, and other heavenly things that we had almost forgotten the taste of. At Imbros, too, you were free from shell fire, and drilled every day just as you did in training. It was whispered, too, but scornfully discredited, that Imbros boasted shower baths, and ovens for the disinfecting of clothing. Others claimed that the Royal Scots had been withdrawn from the Peninsula and were going to the Western front. They were the first regiment to leave of the Twenty-ninth Division. The whole division was to be withdrawn gradually. The Twenty-ninth was our division, and we were to go with it to England. We were to winter in Scotland and after we had been recruited up to full strength were to go to France in the spring. An examination of the empty dugouts strengthened this belief. Blankets, rubber sheets, belts, pieces of equipment, and even overcoats were lying around. In one of the dugouts I found a copy of the *Odyssey*, and half a dozen other books. A few dugouts away I came upon one of our fellows gazing regretfully upon an empty whisky bottle. As I approached him, I overheard him murmur abstractedly, "My favourite brand too, my favourite brand." I passed on without interrupting him. It was too sacred a moment.

CHAPTER 4

Dugouts

The afternoon sun poured down steadily on little groups of men preparing dugouts for habitation. I had a good many details to attend to before I could look about for a suitable place for a dugout. Men had to be told off for different fatigues. Men for pick and shovel work that night were placed in sections so that each group would get as much sleep as possible. All the available dugouts had been taken up by the first comers. The location here was particularly well suited for dugouts. A mule path to the beach ran along the bottom of a narrow ravine. On one side of the path the ground shelved gradually up till it merged into a plain, covered with long grass, overgrown and neglected. On the other side, a ridge sloped up sharply and formed a natural protection before it also merged into a "gorse" covered plateau. Small evergreen bushes served the double purpose of hiding our movements from the enemy and affording some shade from the broiling sun. At the foot of the ridge we made our line of dugouts. The angle of the ridge was so steep that an enemy shell could not possibly drop on our dugouts. A little further away some of A Company's dugouts were in the danger zone. After much hunting, I found a likely looking place. It was about seven feet square, and where I planned to put the head of my dugout a large boulder squatted. It was so eminently suitable that I wondered that no one else had pre-empted it. I took off my equipment, threw my coat on the ground, and began digging. It was soft ground and gave easily.

A short distance away, I could see Art Pratt, digging. He was finding it hard work to make any impression. He saw me, stopped to mop his brow, and grinned cheerfully.

Washing day in war-time

"You should take soft ground like this, Art," I yelled.

"I've gone so far now," said Art, "that it's too late to change," and we resumed our work.

After a few more minutes' digging, my pick struck something that felt like the root of a tree, but I knew there was no tree on that God-forsaken spot large enough to send out big roots. I disentangled the pick and dug a little more, only to find the same obstruction. I took my small entrenching tool, scraped away the dirt I had dug, and began cleaning away near the base of a big boulder. There were no roots there, and gradually I worked away from it. I took my pick again, and at the first blow it stuck. Without trying to disengage it I began straining at it. In a few seconds it began to give, and I withdrew it. Clinging to it was part of a Turkish uniform, from which dangled and rattled the dried-up bones of a skeleton. Nauseated, I hurriedly filled in the place, and threw myself on the ground, physically sick. While I was lying there one of our men came along, searching for a place to bestow himself. He gazed inquiringly at the ground I had just filled in.

"Is there anybody here?" he asked me, indicating the place with a pick-axe.

"Yes," I said, with feeling, "there is."

"It looks to me," he said, "as if some one began digging and then found a better place. If he don't come back soon I'll take it."

For about fifteen minutes he stood there, and I lay regarding him silently. At last he spoke again.

"I think I'll go ahead," he said. "Possession is nine points of the law, and the fellow hasn't been here to claim it."

"I wouldn't if I were you," I said. "That fellow's been there a hell of a long while."

I left him there digging, and crawled away to a safe distance. In a few minutes he passed me.

"Why didn't you tell me?" he demanded, reproachfully.

"Because half of the company saw me digging there and didn't tell me," I said.

I was prospecting around for another place when Art Pratt hailed me. "Why don't you come with me," he said, "instead of digging another place?"

I went to where he was and looked at the dugout. It wasn't

very wide, and I said so. Together we began widening and deepening the dugout, until it was big enough for the two of us. It was gruelling work, but by supper time it was done. The night before, a fatigue party had gone down to the beach and hauled up a big field kitchen. Our cooks had made some tea, and we had been issued some loaves of bread. Art unrolled a large piece of cloth, with all the pomp and ceremony of a man unveiling a monument. He did it slowly and carefully. There was a glitter in his eyes that one associates with an artist exhibiting his masterpiece. He gave a triumphant switch to the last fold and held toward me a large piece of fresh juicy steak!

"Beefsteak!" I gasped. "Sacred beefsteak! Where did you get it?"

Art leaned toward me mysteriously. "Officers' mess," he whispered.

"I've got salt and pepper," I said, "but how are you going to cook it?"

"I don't know," said Art, "but I'm going up to the field kitchen; there's some condensed milk that I may be able to get hold of to spread on our bread."

While Art was gone, I strolled down the ravine a little way to where some of the Royal Engineers were quartered. The Royal Engineers are the men who are looked on in training as a non-combatant force, with safe jobs. In war-time they do no fighting, but their safe jobs consist of such harmless work as fixing up barbed wire in front of the parapet and setting mines under the enemy's trenches. For a rest they are allowed to conduct parties to listening posts and to give the lines for advance saps. Sometimes they make loopholes in the parapet, or bolster up some redoubt that is being shelled to pieces. The Turks were sending over their compliments just as I came abreast of the Engineers' lines. One of the engineers was sifting some gravel when the first shell landed. He dropped the sieve, and turned a back somersault into some gorse-bushes just behind him. The sieve rolled down, swayed from side to side, and settled close to my head, in the depression where I was conscientiously emulating an ostrich. I gathered it to my bosom tenderly and began crawling away. From behind a boulder I heard the engineer bemoaning to an officer the loss of his sieve, and he described in detail how a huge shell had blown it out of his hands. Joyfully I returned to Art with my prize.

59

"What's that for?" said Art.

"Turn it upside down," I said, "and it's a steak broiler."

"Where did you get it?" said Art.

I told him, and related how the engineer had explained it to his officer.

Up at the field kitchen a group was standing around.

"What's the excitement?" I asked Art.

"Those fellows are a crowd of thieves," answered Art, virtuously. "They're looking about to see what they can steal. I was up there a few minutes ago and saw a can of condensed milk lying on the shaft of the field kitchen. They were watching me too closely to give me a chance, but you might be able to get away with it."

The two of us strolled up slowly to where Hebe Wheeler, the creative artist who did our cooking, was holding forth to a critical audience.

"It's all very well to talk about giving you things to eat, but I can't cook pancakes without baking powder. You can't get blood out of a turnip. I'd give you the stuff if I got it to cook, but I don't get it, do I, Corporal?" said Hebe, appealing to me.

I moved over and stood with my back to the shaft on which rested the tin of condensed milk.

"No, Hebe," I said, "you don't get the things; and when you do get them, this crowd steals them on you."

"By God," said Hebe, "that's got to be put a stop to. I'll report the next man I find stealing anything from the cookhouse."

I put my hand cautiously behind my back, until I felt my fingers close on the tin of milk. "You let me know, Hebe," I said, as I slipped the tin into the roomy pocket of my riding breeches, "and I'll make out a crime sheet against the first man whose name you give." I stayed about ten minutes longer talking to Hebe, and then returned to my dugout. Art had finished broiling the piece of steak, and we began our supper. I put my hand in my breeches' pocket to get the milk. Instead of grasping the tin, my fingers closed on a sticky, gluey mass. The tin had been opened when I took it and I had it in my pocket upside down. About half of it had oozed over my pocket. Art was just pouring the remainder on some bread when some one lifted the rubber sheet and stuck his head into our dugout. It was the enraged Hebe Wheeler. As soon as he had missed his precious milk he had made a thorough investigation of all the dugouts. He looked at Art accusingly.

"Come in, Hebe," I said pleasantly. "We don't see you very often."

Hebe paid no attention to my invitation, but glared at Art.

"I've caught you with the goods on," he said. "Give me back that milk, or I'll report you to the platoon officer."

"You can report me to Lord Kitchener if you like," said Art, calmly, as he drained the can; "but this milk stays right here."

Hebe disappeared, breathing vengeance.

After supper that night a crowd sat around the dying embers of one of the fires. This was one of the first positions we had been in where there was cover sufficient to warrant fires being lighted. A mail had been distributed that day, and the men exchanged items of news and swapped gossip. There were men there from all parts of Newfoundland. They spoke in at least thirty different accents. Any one who made a study of it could tell easily from each man's accent the district he came from. Much of the mail was intimate, and necessitated private perusal, but much more was of interest to others. It was interesting to hear a man yell to a friend who came from his same "bay" that another man had enlisted from Robinson's, making up eighteen of the nineteen men of fighting age in the place. Sometimes the news was that "Half has volunteered, and Hed was turned down by the doctor."

This from some resident of the northern parts where the fog is not, and where aspirates are of little consequence. This news gives rise to the opinion that "that's the hend o' Half." This with much discussion and ominous shaking of the head. Sometimes a friend of the absent "Half" would tell of Half's exploit of stealing a trolley from the Reid Newfoundland Railway Company and going twenty miles to see a girl. Sometimes the hero was a married man. Then it was opined that his conjugal relations were not happy, and the reason he enlisted was that "he had heard something." All these opinions and suggestions were voiced with that beautiful freedom from restraint so characteristic of the ordinary conversation of the members of our regiment. Much was made of the arrival of a mail. It did not happen often, and the letters that came were three or four months old. "As cold waters to a thirsty soul," says Solomon, "so is good news from a far country." The Newfoundlanders in that barren, scorched country caught eagerly at every shred of news from that distant Northern country that they loved enough to risk their lives for. With such a setting it is little wonder that the talk was much of home. Behind the persiflage of the talk there was a poignant longing for those dark, cool forests of pine where the caribou roam, and the broad-bosomed lakes and rivers that were the highways for the monsters of the Northern forests on their journey to the mills. The lumbermen of Notre Dame Bay and Green Bay told fearsome and wondrous tales of driving and swamping, of teaming and landing, until one almost heard the blows of the axe, the "gee" and "haw" of the teamsters, and smelt the pungent odour of new-cut pine. The Reid Newfoundland Railway, the single narrow gage road that twists a picturesque trail across the Island, had given largely of its personnel toward the making of the regiment. Firemen and engineers, brakemen and conductors, talked reminiscently of forced runs to catch expresses with freight and accommodation trains. There is an interesting tale of two drivers who blew their whistles in the Morse code, and kept up communication with each other, until a girl learned the code and broke up the friendship. A steamship fireman contributed his quota with a story of labouring through mountainous seas against furious tides when the stokers' utmost efforts served only to keep steamers from losing way. By comparison with the homeland, Turkey suffered much; and the things they said about Gallipoli were lamentable. From the gloom on the other side of the fire a voice chanted softly, "*It's a long, long way to Tipperary, It's a long way to go.*" Gradually all joined in. After Tipperary, came many marching songs. "*Are we downhearted? NO,*" with every one booming out the "No." "*Boys in Khaki, Boys in Blue,*" and at last their own song; to the tune of "*There is a tavern in the town.*"

And when those Newfoundlanders start to yell, start to yell:
Oh, Kaiser Bill, you'll wish you were in hell, were in hell;
For they'll hang you high to your Potsdam palace wall,
You're a damn poor Kaiser, after all.

The singing died down slowly. The talk turned to the trenches and the chances of victory, and by degrees to personal impressions.

"I'd like to know," said one chap, "why we all enlisted."

"When I enlisted," said a man with an accent reminiscent of the Placentia Bay, "I thought there'd be lots of fun, but with weather like this, and nothing fit to eat, there's not much poetry or romance in war any more."

"Right for you, my son," said another; "your King and Country need you, but the trouble is to make your King and Country feed you."

"Don't you wish you were in London now, Gal?" said one chap, turning to me. "You'd have a nice bed to sleep in, and could eat anywhere you liked."

"Well," I said, "enough people tried to persuade me to stop. One fellow told me that the more brains a man had, the farther away he was from the firing-line. He'd been to the front too. I think," I added, "that General Sherman had the right idea."

"I wish you fellows would shut up and go to sleep," said a querulous voice from a nearby dugout.

"You don't know what you're talking about, Gal; General Sherman was an optimist."

"It doesn't do any good to talk about it now," said Art Pratt, in a matter of fact voice. "Some of you enlisted so full of love of country that there was patriotism running down your chin, and some of you enlisted because you were disappointed in love, but the most of you enlisted for love of adventure, and you're getting it."

Again the querulous subterranean voice interrupted: "Go to sleep, you fellows—there's none of you knows what you're talking about. There's only one reason any of us enlisted, and that's pure, low down, unmitigated ignorance." Amid general laughter the class in applied psychology broke up, and distributed themselves in their various dugouts.

Halfway down to my dugout, I was arrested by the sound of scuffling, much blowing and puffing, and finally the satisfied grunt that I knew proceeded from Hebe Wheeler.

"I've got a spy," he yelled. "Here's a bloody Turk."

"Turk nothing," said a disgusted voice. "Don't you know a man from your own company?"

Hebe relinquished his hold on his captive and subsided, grumbling. The other arose, shook himself, and went his way, voicing his opinion of people who built their dugouts flush with the ground.

63

"What do you think of the news from the Western front?" said Art, when I located him.

"What is it?" I asked.

"The enemy are on the run at the Western front. The British have taken four lines of German trenches for a distance of over five miles in the vicinity of Loos. The bulletin board at Brigade headquarters says that they have captured several large guns, a number of machine guns, and seventeen thousand unwounded prisoners. If they can keep this up long enough for the Turks to realize that it is hopeless to expect any help from that quarter, Abdul Pasha will soon give in."

We were talking about Abdul Pasha's surrendering when we dropped off to sleep. We must have been asleep about two hours when the insistent, crackling sound of rapid fire, momentarily increasing in volume, brought us to our feet. Away up on the right, where the Australians were, the sky was a red glare from the flashing of many rifles. Against this, we could see the occasional flare of different coloured rockets that gave the warships their signals for shelling. Very soon one of our officers appeared.

"Stand to arms for the Newfoundlanders," he said.

"What is it?" I asked.

"The Australians are advancing," he answered. "We'll go up as reinforcements if we're needed. Tell your men to put on their ammunition belts, and have their rifles ready. They needn't put on their packs; but keep them near them so that they can slip them on if we get the order to move away."

I went about among the men of my section, passing along the word. Everybody was tingling with excitement. Nobody knew just what was about to happen; but every one thought that whatever it was it would prove interesting. For about half an hour the rapid fire kept up, then by degrees died down.

"Did you see that last rocket?" said a man near me; "that means they've done it. A red rocket means that the navy is to fire, a green to continue firing, and a white one means that we've won."

In a few minutes Mr. Nunns walked toward us. "You can put your equipments off, and turn in again," he said, "nothing doing tonight."

"What is all the excitement?" I asked.

"Oh, it's the Anzacs again," he said; "when they heard of the advance at Loos, they went over across, and surprised the Turks. They've taken two lines of trenches. They did it without any orders—just wanted to celebrate the good news."

I was awakened the next morning by the sound of a whizz-bang flying over our dugout. Johnny Turk was sending us his best respects. I shook Art, who was sleeping heavily.

"Get up, Art," I said. I might as well have spoken to a stone wall. I tried again. Putting my mouth to his ear, I shouted, "Stand to, Art. Stand to."

Art turned over, sleeping. "I'll stand three if you like, but don't disturb me," he muttered, and relapsed into coma.

In a few minutes, two or three more shells came along. They were well over the ridge behind us, but were landing almost in the midst of another line of dugouts. I stood gazing at them for a little while. A man passed me running madly. "Come on," he gasped, "and yell for the stretcher." I followed him without further question. "It's all right," he said, slowing up just before we came to the line of dugouts that had just been shelled. "They've got him all right." We continued toward a group that crowded about a stretcher. A man was lying on it, with his head raised on a haversack. He rolled his eyes slowly and surveyed the group. "What the hell is the matter?" he said dazedly; then felt himself over gingerly for wounds. Apparently he could find none. "What hit me?" he asked, appealing to a grinning Red Cross man.

"Nothing," said the other, "except about a ton of earth. It's a lucky thing some one saw you. That last shell buried you alive."

The whistle of a coming shell dispersed the grinning spectators. I went back to my dugout, and found Art busily toasting some bread over the sieve that I had commandeered the day before.

"What was the excitement?" he asked.

"Charlie Renouf," I said, "was buried alive."

"Heavens," said Art, "he's the postman; we can't afford to lose him. That reminds me that I've got to write some letters."

After we had finished breakfast, Art produced some writing paper and an indelible pencil. I did not have any writing paper, but I contributed a supply of service postcards, that bear such meagre information as "I am quite well," "I am sick," "I am wounded," "I

Cleaning up after coming down from the trenches at Suvla

am in hospital and doing well," "I am in hospital and expect to be discharged soon," "I have not heard from you for a long time," "I have had no letter from you since—," "I have your letter of—," "I have received your parcel of—," and a space for the date and the signature. When a man writes home from the front, he crosses out all but the sentences he wants read, puts in the date, and adds his signature. This is the ordinary means of communication. About once a week a man is allowed to write some letters; but these are censored by his platoon officer, who seals them, and signs his name as a record of their having been passed by him. Sometimes the censor at the base opens a few of them. Perhaps once a fortnight a few privileged characters are given large blue envelopes, that have printed in the corner:

Note

Correspondence in this envelope need not be censored regimentally. The contents are liable to examination at the Base. The following Certificate must be signed by the writer:

I certify on my honour that the contents of this envelope refer to nothing but private and family matters.

Signature

(Name only)

While we were writing, the orderly sergeant, that dread of loafers, who appoints all details for fatigue work, bore down upon our dugout. "Two men from you, Corporal Gallishaw," he said, "for bomb throwers. Give me their names as soon as you can. They're for practice this afternoon."

"One here, right away," said Art, "and put Lew O'Dea down for the other."

Lew O'Dea was a character. He was in the next dugout to me. The first day on the Peninsula, his rifle had stuck full of sand, and some one had stolen his tin canteen for cooking food. He immediately formed himself into an anti-poverty society of one thereafter, and went around like a walking arsenal. I never saw him with fewer than three rifles, usually he carried half a dozen. He always kept two or three of them spotlessly clean; so that no matter when rifle inspection came, he always had at least one to show. He had been a little late in getting his rifle clean once and was determined not to be caught any more. His equipment always contained a varied assortment of canteens, seven or eight gas masks, and his dugout was luxurious with rubber sheets and blankets. "I inherited them," he always answered, whenever anybody questioned him about them. With ammunition for his several rifles, when he started for the trenches in full marching order, he carried a load that a mule need by no means have been ashamed of.

"Do you want to go on bomb throwing detail this afternoon?" I called to O'Dea across the top of the dugout.

"Sure," he answered; "does a swim want to duck?"

"Fine," I said; "report here at two o'clock."

At two o'clock, accompanied by an officer and a sergeant, we went down the road a little way to where some Australians were conducting a class in bomb throwing. A brown-faced chap from Sydney showed me the difference between bombs that you explode by lighting a match, bombs that are started by pulling out a plug, and the dinky little three-second "cricket balls" that explode by pressing a spring. I asked him about the attack the night before. He told me that they had been for some time waiting for a chance to make a local advance that would capture an important redoubt in the Turkish line. Every night at exactly nine o'clock, the Navy had thrown a searchlight on the part of the line the Anzacs wanted to capture. For ten minutes they kept up heavy firing. Then, after a ten minutes' interval of darkness and suspended firing, they began a second illumination and bombardment, commencing always at twenty minutes past nine, and ending precisely at half past. After a little while, the enemy, knowing just the exact minute the bombardment was to begin, took the first beam of the searchlight as a hint to clear out. But the night before, a crowd of eager Australians had crept softly along in the shadow made doubly dark by the glare of the searchlight, the noise of their advance covered by the sound of the bombardment. As soon as the bombardment ceased and the searchlight's beam was succeeded by darkness, they poured into the Turkish position. They had taken the astonished Turks completely by surprise.

"We didn't expect to make the attack for another week," said the Australian; "but as soon as our boys heard that we were winning in France, they thought they'd better start something. There hasn't been any excitement over our way now for a long time," he said. "I'm about fed up on this waiting around the trenches." He fingered one of the little cricket-ball bombs caressingly. "Think of it," he said; "all you do is press that little spring, and three seconds after you're a casualty."

"Pressing that little spring," said I, "is my idea of nothing to do, unless you're a particularly fast sprinter."

"By the Lord Harry, Newfoundland," said the Australian, with a peculiar, excited glint in his eye, "that's an inspiration."

"What's an inspiration?" I asked, in bewilderment.

The Australian stretched himself on the ground beside me, resting his chin in his cupped hands. "When I was in Sydney," he said slowly and thoughtfully, "I did a hundred yards in ten seconds easily. Now if I can get in a traverse that's only eight or nine yards long, and press the spring of one of those little cricket balls, I ought to be able to get out on the other side of the traverse before it explodes." Art and Lew O'Dea passed along just then and I jumped up to go with them. "Don't forget to look for me if you're over around the Fifteenth Australians," said the Australian. "Ask for White George."

"I won't forget," I said, as I hurried away to join the others.

We were about half way to our dugouts when we passed a string of our men carrying about twenty mail bags. It was the second instalment of a lot of mail that had been landed the day before. We followed the sweating carriers up the road to the quarter-master sergeant's dugout, and waited around humbly while that autocrat leisurely sorted out the mail, making remarks about each letter and waiting after each remark for the applause he felt it deserved. With maddening deliberation he scanned each address. "Corporal W.P. Costello." "He's at the base," some one answered. Corporal Costello's letter was put aside. "Private George Butler." Private Butler, on the edge of the crowd, pushed and elbowed his way toward the quarter-master sergeant. "Here you are; letter for Butler." The august Q.M.S. placed the letter beside his elbow. "Wait till the lot's sorted, and you'll get them all together." Private Butler, with ill-restrained impatience, resumed his place on the outside. After the letters, the parcels had to be sorted. Some enterprising person at the base had opened a lot of them. One fellow received a large box of cigarettes that he would have enjoyed smoking if the man at the base had not seen them first. Art Pratt drew a lot of mail, including a parcel, intact except for the contents. A diligent search in a box a foot square failed to locate anything more than a pair of socks, which Art presented to me with his compliments. Some papers, two months old, with some casualty lists of the First Newfoundland Regiment, had no address; the wrapper had gone before, somewhere between Newfoundland and the Dardanelles. Everybody claimed the papers. Various proofs were offered to show the ownership. One fellow knew by the way they were rolled up that they were from his family. Another, more original than the rest, was certain they were his, because he had written for papers of those dates, in order to see the announcement of the casualty of a friend. It was pointed out derisively that a letter written after that casualty had occurred would only then have reached Newfoundland; and to get a lot of papers in reply would be a physical impossibility. The claimant, in no wise abashed, suggested that lots be drawn. This was pooh-poohed. At last, to avoid discussion, the quarter-master sergeant took the papers himself, and put them in his greatcoat. "I'll distribute them after I've read them," he announced, and pulled the rubber sheet across the top of his dugout, as a delicate hint that the interview was finished. The crowd slowly melted away. I received one letter, and was sitting on the edge of my dugout reading it when one of our men passing along, yelled to me. "Hey," he said, "you come from the United States, don't you?"

"Yes," I said; "what do you want to know that for?"

"I've got something here," he said, stopping, "that comes from there too." He dived into his pocket, and produced a medley of articles. From these he selected a small paper-wrapped parcel.

"What's that?" I said.

"It's chewing gum," he answered; "real American chewing gum like the girls chew in the subway in New York." He unwrapped it, selected a piece, placed it in his mouth, and began chewing it with elaborated enjoyment. After a few minutes, he came nearer. "By golly," he said, with an exaggerated nasal drawl, "it's good gum, I'll soon begin to feel like a blooming Yank. I'm talking like a Yank already. Don't you wish you had some of this?"

"I'll make you a sporting offer," I answered. "I'll fight you for the rest of what you've got."

"No, you won't," he answered nasally; "it's made me feel exactly like a Yank; I'm too proud to fight."

CHAPTER 5

Waiting For the War to Cease

We were still in dugouts when Art Pratt woke me one morning with a vicious kick, to show me my boots lying outside of the dugout, filled with rain water. All the night before it had poured steadily, but now it was clearing nicely. The island of Imbros, fifteen miles away, that seemed to draw a great deal nearer before every rainstorm, had retreated to its normal position. The sky was still gray, but it was the leaden gray of a Turkish autumn day. From Suvla Bay the wind blew keen and piercing. I salved the boots from the rain puddle, emptied them, dried them out as best I could with my *puttees*, and put them on. Art, in his own inimitable way, said unprintable things about a rifle that had been left outside, and that now necessitated laborious cleaning, in time for rifle inspection. All through breakfast, Lew O'Dea elaborated on the much-quoted remarks of the Governor of North Carolina to the Governor of South Carolina. Rum had not been issued as per schedule the evening before. Art began a maliciously fabricated story of a conversation he had heard in which a senior officer had stated that now that the cold weather had come, there would be no more rum. Just then, some one shouted, to "Look up in the sky." From the direction of the trenches a dark cloud was coming rapidly toward us. (A few nights before, while we were in trenches, we had been ordered to put on our gas masks; for, a little to the right of us, the Turks had turned the poison gas on the Ghurkhas.) At first, the dark mass in the sky appeared to some to be poison gas. They immediately dived for their gas masks. As it came nearer, however, we were able to distinguish that it was not a cloud, but a huge flock of wild geese, beginning their southern

71

migration. O'Dea selected a rifle from his collection, loaded it, and waited till the geese were almost directly overhead; then, amid derisive cheering, he fired ten rounds at them. They were much too high in air for a successful shot, even if he had used gunshot; but even after they were almost over Imbros Island, Lew continued firing. When an officer arrived, demanding sarcastically if Lew O'Dea wouldn't sooner send some written invitations to the Turks to shell us, he subsided, and began cleaning his artillery. Until then, we had been wearing thin khaki duck uniforms with short pants that made us look like boy scouts. We had found these rather cool at night; but in the hot days we preferred them to the heavy khaki drill uniforms that were kept in kit bags at the beach. I had landed without a kit bag, and the change of uniform I kept in the pack I carried on my back. A little while before, I had put on the heavy uniform and thrown away the light weight one. On the Peninsula, when you have to walk with all your possessions on your back, each additional ounce counts for much. As soon as we found that it was impossible to get water to wash or shave in, we threw away our towels and soap. A few kept their razors. The only thing I hung on to was my tooth brush—not for its legitimate purpose, but to clean the sand and grit out of my rifle.

"Go over and ask Mr. Nunns," said Art to me, while we were cleaning our rifles, "if he'll give us a pass to go down to the beach to find my kit bag. I'll finish cleaning your rifle while you go over." I handed the rifle to Art, and went over to look for Mr. Nunns. When I found him he was censoring some letters.

"You'd better wait till this afternoon, before going," he said. "I want you to take twenty men and carry up ten boxes of ammunition to the firing line, where A Company are. They're coming out to-morrow night and we're to relieve them." He gave me a pass, and I took it over to Art.

"You can go down this morning if you like," I said, "or you can wait till I get back from this ammunition detail."

"If you're not later than two o'clock," said Art, "I'll wait for you."

I found the detail of twenty men for ammunition-carrying waiting for me near the field kitchen. We crawled cautiously along some open ground, past the quarter-master's dugout and the dugouts that were dignified by the name of orderly room, where the colonel and adjutant conducted the clerical business of the battalion, issued daily orders, and sentenced defaulters. "Napoleon knew what was what," said the man near me, as he wriggled along, "when he said that an army fights on its stomach. I've been on my stomach half the time since I've been in Gallipoli." We straightened up when we came to the communication trench that gave us cover from snipers. Ordinarily we walked upright when we were behind the lines, but for a few days past enemy snipers had been extraordinarily active. The Turkish snipers were the most effective part of their organization. Each sniper was armed with a rifle with telescopic sights. With a rifle so equipped, a good shot can hit a man at seven hundred yards, just as easily as the ordinary soldier can shoot at one hundred.

The ten boxes of ammunition were very heavy, and the heat of the day necessitated a great many rests, before we reached the part of the line held by A Company. A Company had been losing heavily for a day or two because of snipers. A couple of the men were talking about it when I came along.

"I don't see," one of them was saying, "how they can get us at night."

"It's this way," explained the other. "The cigarette makers send their snipers out sometime at night. Instead of going back that night they stay out for a week, or longer. All the ration Johnny Turk needs is a swallow of water, some onions, or olives, and a biscuit or two."

"How is it," I asked, "we don't see them in the daytime?"

"It's this way," said the A Company man. "He paints himself, his rifle, and his clothes green. Then he twists some twigs and branches around him and kids you he's a tree."

"The way they do in this part of the trench," said another man who had been listening to the conversation, "is to work in pairs. They get a dugout somewhere where they can get a pretty good view of our trenches. They see where we move about most, and aim their machine gun at the top of the parapet. Then they clamp it down. At night when the sentries are posted, they simply press the trigger, and there are some more casualties."

"You've got to hand it to Johnny Turk, just the same," said the first man. "One of them will stand up in his dugout in broad daylight, exposed from his waist up, and give you a chance to pot him, so that his mate can get you. We used to lose men that way first. As soon as we aimed, the second sniper turned his machine gun on us and got our man. Now we've found a better way. We stick a helmet up on top of a rifle just above the parapet, and fire from another part of the trench."

"We've been having trouble with them down in dugouts," I said. "Some of the fellows say it's stray bullets, but it seems to me that they're going too fast to be spent. You can tell a bullet that's spent by the sound."

One of the A Company sergeants who had been listening to the discussion joined in. "It's snipers all right," he said. "It's easy enough for a German officer to get into our trenches. Men are coming in all the time from working parties, and night patrols, and the engineers go back and forth every hour or so fixing up the barb wire. Only a little while ago they found one fellow. He had stripped a uniform from one of our dead, dressed himself in it, and walked up to our parapet one night. The sentry didn't know the difference, because the other fellow spoke good English, so he let him pass. All they have to do is say 'What ho,' or, 'Where's the Dublin's section of trench?' They can get by all right."

The officer to whom I had delivered the ammunition sent word that it had been checked and that we could return to our company. We were only a short distance down the communication trench when a party of officers came along. We drew a little to one side, and stopped to let them pass. Not one of them was under the rank of lieutenant-colonel, and one of them was a general. He was a rather tall, spare man, with a drooping brown moustache. He was most unlike the usual type of gruff, surly general officers in charge. His eyes had a kindly, friend-of-the-family sort of twinkle. His type was more like a superintendent of construction, or a kindly old family physician. "Look at the ribbons on the old boy's chest," said the man near me. "He's got enough medals to make a keel for a battleship." In the British army, those who have seen previous service wear on the breast of their tunics the ribbons for each campaign. The general halted his red-tabbed staff where we stood.

"Are you Newfoundlanders, Corporal?" he said to me.

"Yes, sir," I answered.

LANDING BRITISH TROOPS FROM THE TRANSPORTS AT THE DARDANELLES UNDER THE PROTECTION OF THE BATTLESHIPS

"They've made it pretty warm for you since you've been here," he added, with a smile. "Your men are most efficient trench diggers. If I had an army like them, we'd dig our way to Constantinople." With that he passed on with a smile. A pompous-looking sergeant brought up the rear of the general's escort.

"Who was that, that just spoke to us, Sergeant?" I asked.

The sergeant surveyed me contemptuously. "Is it possible that you don't know 'im. 'E's General Sir Ian Hamilton, General Commander-in-Chief of the Mediterranean Force, 'e is."

General Sir Ian Hamilton has won the unquestioned devotion of the First Newfoundland Regiment. Many times after that, he visited the front line trenches and stopped to exchange a few words with men here and there. It is a curious thing that while the young subaltern lieutenants held themselves very much aloof, the senior officers chatted amiably with our men. The Newfoundlanders, democratic to the core, hated anything that in the least savoured of "side," and they admired the courage of a general officer who took his chances in the firing line.

Art was waiting for me when I reached the dugout after my ammunition fatigue. I accompanied him down the mule path that led along the edge of the Salt Lake to West Beach, where we had made our landing the first night. The place looked very different now. Under the shelter of the beetling cliffs, the engineers had constructed dugouts of all sorts. The beach was piled high with boxes of beef, biscuits, jam, lime juice, and rum. At the top of the hill, a temporary dressing station for the wounded had been built; and nearer the beach was a clearing station, from which the wounded were taken by motor ambulance to the hospital ship. At different points along the beach, piers had been built for the landing of supplies and troops, and for the loading of wounded into lighters to be taken to the hospital ships waiting out in deeper water. The Australians had put up a wire fence around a part of beach and used it for a graveyard. We found the man in charge of the kit bags of the Newfoundlanders, and after much search located Art's bag, and took out the stuff we wanted. On the way back, in a little ravine just on the edge of the Salt Lake, we came upon two horsemen. They were General Hamilton and his aide. The general returned our salute smilingly.

"Who is it?" said Art.

"It's Sir Ian Hamilton," I said. "Doesn't he look like the sort of man it would be wise to confide in?"

"Yes, he does," said Art. "Evidently he has confidence in our troops' ability to hold their own," added Art. "The Turks have four lines of trenches to fall back on; we have only one firing line."

There was the same group around the field kitchen when we arrived back at our lines. They were swapping yarns and telling stories with a lurid intermixture of profanity and a liberal sprinkling of trench slang. To me, one of the most interesting side lights of the war is the slang that forms a great part of the vocabulary of the trenches. Early morning tea, when we got it, was "gun-fire." A Turk was never a Turk. He was a Turkey, Abdul Pasha, or a cigarette maker. A regiment is a "mob." A psychologist would have been interested to see that nobody ever spoke of a comrade as having died or been killed, but had "gone west." All the time I was at the front, I never heard one of our men say that another had been killed. A man who was killed in our regiment had "lost his can," although this referred most particularly to men shot through the head. Ordinarily a dead man was called a "washout"; or it was said that he had "copped it." The caution to keep your head down always came, "Keep your napper down low." To get wounded with one of our own bullets was to get a "dose of three-o-three." The bullet has a diameter of three-hundred-and-three thousandths of an inch.

Mr. Nunns came toward the group, looking for Stenlake. It was Sunday afternoon, and he thought it would be well to have a service. Stenlake was found, and a crowd trailed after him to an empty dugout, where he gathered them about him and began. It was a simple, sincere service. Out there in that barren country, it seemed a strange thing to see those rough men gathered about Stenlake while he read a passage or led a hymn. But it was most impressive. The service was almost over, and Stenlake was offering a final prayer, when the Turkish batteries opened fire. Ordinarily at the first sound of a shell, men dived for shelter; but gathered around that dugout, where a single shell could have wrought awful havoc, not a man stirred. They stayed motionless, heads bowed reverently, until Stenlake had finished. Then quietly they dispersed. As a lesson in faith it was most illuminating.

It was strange to see week by week the psychological change that had come over the men. Most of all I noticed it in the songs they sang. At first the songs had been of a boisterous character, that foretold direful things that would happen to the Kaiser and his family "*As we go marching through Germany.*" These had all given place to songs that voiced to some extent the longing for home that possessed these voluntary exiles. "*I want to go back to Michigan*" was a favourite. Perhaps even more so was "*The little gray home in the West.*" "*Tipperary*" was still in demand, not because of the lilt of a march that it held, but for the pathetic little touch of "*my heart's right there,*" and perhaps for the reference to "*the sweetest girl I know.*"

Perhaps it may have been the effect of Stenlake's service, or it may have been the news that we were to go into the firing line the next day, that made the men seek their dugouts early that Sunday evening. But there was something heavy in the air that night. For almost a week we had been comparatively safe in dugouts. Tomorrow we were again to go into the firing line and wait impotently while our number was reduced gradually but pitilessly. The hopelessness of the thing seemed clearer that evening than any other time we had been there. Simpson, "the Man with the Donkeys," had been killed that day. After a whole summer in which he seemed to be impervious to bullets, a stray bullet had caught him in the heart on his way down Shrapnel Valley with a consignment of wounded. Simpson had been so much a part of the Peninsular life that it was hard to realize that he had gone to swell the list of heroes that Australia has so much cause to be proud of. A Company had suffered heavily in the front line trenches that day. A number of stretchers had passed down the road that ran in front of our dugouts, with A Company men for the dressing station on the beach. Snipers had been busy. From the A Company stretcher-bearers came news that others had been killed. One piece of news filtered slowly down to us that evening, that had an unaccountably strange effect on the men of B Company. Sam Lodge had been killed. Sam Lodge was perhaps the most widely known man in the whole regiment. There were very few Newfoundlanders who did not think kindly of the big, quiet, reliable looking college man. He had enlisted at the very first call for volunteers. Other men had been killed that day; and since the regiment had been at Gallipoli, men had stood by while their dugout mates were torn by shrapnel or sank down moaning, with a sniper's bullet in the brain; but nothing had ever had the same effect, at any rate on the men of our company, as the news that Sam Lodge had been killed that day. Perhaps it was that everybody knew him. Other nights men had crowded around the fire, telling stories, exchanging gossip, or singing. To-night all was quiet; there was not even the sound of men creeping about from dugout to dugout, visiting chums. Suddenly, from away up on the extreme right end of the line of dugouts, came the sound of a clear tenor voice, singing, "T*enting To-night on the Old Camp Ground.*" Never have I heard anything so mournful. It is impossible to describe the penetrating pathos of the old Civil War song. Slowly the singer continued, amidst a profound hush. His voice sank, until one could scarcely catch the words when he sang, "*Waiting for the war to cease.*" At last he finished. There was scarcely a stir, as the men dropped off to sleep.

It was a quiet, sober lot of men who filed into a shady, tree-dotted ravine the next day behind the stretcher that bore the remains of Private Sam Lodge. Stenlake read the burial service. Everybody who could turned out to pay their last respects to the best liked man in the regiment. After the brief service, Colonel Burton, the commanding officer, Captain Carty, Lodge's company commander, a group of senior and junior officers, and a number of profoundly affected soldiers gathered about the grave while the body was lowered into it. In the shade of a spreading tree, within sound of the mournful wash of the tide in Suvla Bay, lies poor Sam Lodge, a good, cheerful soldier, uncomplaining always, a man whose last thought was for others. "Don't bother to lift me down off the parapet, boys," he had said when he was hit; "I'm finished."

CHAPTER 6

No Man's Land

Our dugouts were located about a quarter of a mile inland from the edge of the Salt Lake. Somewhere at the other side of the Salt Lake was the cleverly concealed landing place of the aeroplane service. Commander Sampson, who had been in action since the beginning of the war, was in charge of the aeroplane squadron. One day, by clever manoeuvring he forced one of the enemy planes, a Taube, away from its own lines and back over the Salt Lake. Here after a spectacular fight in mid air, Sampson forced the other to surrender and captured his machine. The Taube he thereafter used for daily reconnaissance. Every afternoon we watched him hover over the Turkish lines, circle clear of their bursting shrapnel, poising long enough to complete his observations, then return to the Salt Lake with his report for our artillery and the navy. The day after Sam Lodge's burial, we watched two hostile 'planes chase Sampson back right to our trenches. When they came near enough, our men opened rapid fire that forced them to turn; but before Sampson reached his landing place at Salt Lake, we could see that he was in trouble. One of the wings of his machine was drooping badly. From the other side of the Salt Lake, a motor ambulance was tearing along towards the place where he was expected to land. The Taube sank gradually to the ground, the ambulance drew up to within about thirty feet of it, and turned about, waiting. We saw Sampson jump out of his seat, almost before the machine touched the ground, and walk to the waiting ambulance. The ambulance had just started, when a shell from a Turkish gun hit the prostrate aeroplane and tore a large hole in it. With marvellous precision, the Turkish battery pumped

80

three or four shells almost on top of the first. In a few minutes, all that was left of the Taube was a twisted mass of frame work; of the wings, not a fragment remained.

But although Sampson had lost his 'plane, he had completed his mission. About half an hour later, the navy in the bay began a bombardment. We could see the men-o'-war lined up, pouring broadsides over our heads into the Turkish trenches. First, we saw the gray ships calmly riding the waves; then, from their sides came puffs of whitish gray smoke, and the flash of the discharge, followed by the jarring report of the explosion. Around the bend of Anafarta Bay, we saw creeping in a strange, low-lying, awkward-looking craft that reminded one of the barges one sees used for dredging harbours. It was one of the new monitors, the most efficiently destructive vessel in the navy. Soon the artillery on the land joined in. About four o'clock the bombardment had started; and all that afternoon the terrific din kept up. When we went into the firing line that evening at dark, the bombardment was still going on. About nine o'clock it stopped; but at three the next morning, it was resumed with even greater force. The part of the line we were holding was in a valley; to the right and left of us, the trenches ran up hill. From our position in the middle, we had a splendid view of the other parts of the line. All that morning the bombardment kept up. Our gunners were concentrating on the trenches well up the hill on the left. First we watched our shells demolish the enemy's front line trench. Immense shells shrieked through the air above our heads and landed in the Turks' firing line. Gradually but surely the huge projectiles battered down the enemy defences. The Turks stuck to their ground manfully, but at last they had to give up. Through field glasses we could see the communication trenches choked with fleeing Turks. Some of our artillery, to prevent their escape, concentrated on the support trenches. This manoeuvre served a double purpose: besides preventing the escape of those retreating from the battered front line trench, it stopped reinforcements from coming up. Still farther back, a mule train bringing up supplies, was caught in open ground in the curtain of fire. The Turks, caught between two fires, could not escape. In a short time all that was left of the scientifically constructed entrenchments was a conglomerate heap of sand bags, equipments, and machine guns; and on top of it all lay the mangled bodies of men and mules.

All through the bombardment, we had hoped for the order to go over the parapet. When we had been rushed to the firing line the night before, we thought it was to take part in the attack. Instead of this, we were held in the firing line. For the Worcesters on our left was reserved the distinction of making the charge. High explosives cleared the way for their advance, and cheering and yelling they went over parapet. The Turks in the front line trenches, completely demoralized, fled to the rear. A few, too weak or too sorely wounded to run, surrendered. While the bombardment was going on, our men stood in their trenches, craning their necks over the parapet. All through the afternoon, the excitement was intense. Men jumped up and down, running wildly from one point in the trench to another to get a better view. Some fired their rifles in the general direction of the enemy; "just a few joy guns," they said. Everybody was laughing and shouting delightedly. Down in the bay, the gray ships looked almost as small as launches in the mist formed by the smoke of the guns. The Newfoundlanders might have been a crowd rooting at a baseball game. Every few minutes, when the smoke in the bay cleared sufficiently to reveal to us a glimpse of the ships, the trenches resounded to the shouts of, "Come on, the navy," and "Good old Britain." And when the great masses of iron hurtled through the air and tore up sections of the enemy's parapet, we shouted delightedly, "Iron rations for Johnny Turk!"

Prisoners taken in this engagement told us that the Turkish rank and file heartily hated their German officers. From the first, they had not taken kindly to underground warfare. The Turks were accustomed to guerrilla fighting, and had to be driven into the trenches by the German officers at the point of their revolvers. One prisoner said that he had been an officer; but since the beginning of the campaign, he had been replaced by a German. At that time, he told us, the Turks were officered entirely by Germans. For two or three days after that, at short intervals, one or two at a time, Turks dribbled in to surrender. They were tired of fighting, they said, and were almost starved to death. Many more would surrender, they told us, but they were kept back by fear of being shot by their German officers.

With the monotony varied occasionally by some local engagement like this, we dragged through the hot, fly-pestered days, and cold, draughty, vermin-infested nights of September and early October. By the middle of October, disease and scarcity of water had depleted our ranks alarmingly. Instead of having four days on the firing line and eight days' rest, we were holding the firing line eight days and resting only four. In my platoon, of the six non-commissioned officers who had started with us, only two corporals were left, one other and I. For a week after the doctor had ordered him to leave the Peninsula, the other corporal hung on, pluckily determined not to leave me alone. All this time, the work of the platoon was divided between us; he stayed up half the night, and I the other half. At last, he had to be personally conducted to the clearing station.

Just about the middle of October comes a Mohammedan feast that lasts for three or four days. During the days of the feast, while our battalion was in the firing line, some prisoners who surrendered told us that the Turks were suffering severely from lack of food and warm clothing. All sorts of rumours ran through the trench. One was that some one had reliable information that the supreme commander of the Turkish forces had sent to Berlin for men to reinforce his army. If the reinforcements did not come in four days, he would surrender his entire command. Men ordered off the Peninsula by the medical officer, instead of proceeding to the clearing station, sneaked back to their positions in the trench, waiting to see the surrender. But the surrender never came. Things went on in the same old dreary, changeless round. More than sickness, or bullets, the sordid monotony had begun to tell on the men. Every day, officers were besieged with requests for permission to go out between the lines to locate snipers. When men were wanted for night patrol, for covering parties, or for listening post details, every one volunteered. Ration parties to the beach, which had formerly been a dread, were now an eagerly sought variation, although it was a certainty that from every such party we should lose ten per cent. of the personnel. Any change, of any sort, was welcome. The thought of being killed had lost its fear. Daily intercourse with death had robbed it of its horror. Here was one case where familiarity had bred contempt.

Most of the men had sunk into apathy, simply waiting for the day their turn was to come, wondering how soon would come the bullet that had on it their "name and number." Most of the men in talking to each other, especially to their sick comrades, spoke hopefully of the outcome; but those I talked with alone all had the same thought: only by a miracle could they escape alive; that miracle was a "cushy one."

One wave of hope swept over the Peninsula in that dreary time. The brigade bulletin board contained the news that it was expected that in a day or two at the most Bulgaria would come into the war on the side of the Allies. To us this was of tremendous importance. With a frontier bordering on Turkey, Bulgaria might turn the scale in our favour. Life became again full of possibilities and interest. Our interpreters printed up an elaborate menu in Turkish that recited the various good things that might be found in our trenches by Turks who would surrender. At the foot of the menus was a little note suggesting that now was the ideal time to come in, and that the ideal way to celebrate the feast was to become our guests. These menus we attached to little stakes and just in front of the Turkish barbed wire we stuck them in the ground. Several Turks came in within the next few days, but whether as a result of this or not, it was impossible to say. The feeling of renewed hope and buoyancy caused by the news of the imminence of Bulgaria's alliance with us was of short duration. A day or so afterwards came the alarming news that the Allied ministers had left Bulgaria; and the following day came word that Bulgaria had joined in the war, not with us, but with the Central Powers. Again apathy settled on the men. Now, too, the rainy season had set in in earnest. Torrents of rain poured down daily on the trenches, choking the drains, and filling the passageway with thick gray mud in which one slipped and floundered helplessly, and which coated uniforms and equipments like cement. One relief it did bring with it. Men who had not had a bath, or a shave in months, were able to collect in their rubber sheets enough rain water to wash and shave with. But the drinking water was still scarce. On other parts of the Peninsula there was plenty of it; but we had so few men available for duty that we could scarcely spare enough men to go for it. Also, there was the difficulty in securing proper receptacles for its conveyance. Most of the men were very much exhausted, and the trip of four or five miles for water would have been too much for them. Even when we did get water, it had to be boiled to kill the germs of disease, and to prevent men from being poisoned. The boiled water was flat and tasteless; and to counteract this, we were given a spoonful of lime juice about once a week. This we put in our water bottles. About every third day we were issued some rum. Twice a week, an officer appeared in the trench carrying a large stone jar bearing the magic letters in black paint, P.D.R., Pure Demerara Rum. This he doled out as if every drop had cost a million dollars. Each man received just enough to cover the bottom of his canteen, not more than an eighth of a tumbler. Just before going out on any sort of night fatigue on the wet ground, it was particularly grateful. We had long ago given up reckoning time by the calendar, and days either were or were not "Rum days." Men who were wounded on these days bequeathed their share to their particular pals or to their dugout mates. Some of the men were total abstainers with the courage of their convictions; they steadfastly refused to touch it. The other men canvassed these on rum days for their share of the fiery liquid, and in exchange did the temperance men's share of fatigue duty. During this time, there was very little fighting. Both sides were entrenched and prepared to stay there for the winter. In the particular section of trench we held, we knew that any attempt at an advance would be hopeless and suicidal. The ground in front was too well commanded by enemy machine guns. Still, we thought that some other parts of the line might advance and turn one of the flanks of the enemy. Nothing was impossible to the Dublins or the Munsters; and there was always faith in the invincible Australians. We could not forget the way the Australians a short time before had celebrated the news of the British advance at Loos.

Just after the Turkish feast, we went into dugouts again for a few days, and back once more to the firing line. This time, we were up in the farm house district near Chocolate Hill. It was a place particularly exposed to shell fire; for the old skeletons of farm houses made good targets for the enemy's guns. Every afternoon, the Turks sent over about a dozen or so shells, just to show us that they knew we were there. After Bulgaria came in against us, it seemed to us that the Turks grew much more prodigal of their shells than formerly. Where before they sent over ten, they now fired twenty. It was rather grimly ironic to find, on examination of some of the shell casings, that they were shells made by Great Britain and supplied to the Turks in the Balkan War. There was a certain amount of sardonic satisfaction in knowing that the fortifications on Achi Baba were placed there by British engineers when we looked on the Turks as friends. No. 8 platoon was entrenched just in front of a field in which grew a number of apple trees. In the daytime we could not get to these, but at night some of the more venturesome spirits crawled out and returned with their haversacks full. A little further along was what had once been a garden. Even now there were still growing some tomatoes and some watermelons. The rest of it was a mass of battered stones that had once been fences. Here it was that the old gray bearded farmers who had been peacefully working in their fields had hung up their scythes and taken down from their hook on the wall old rusty muskets and fought in their dooryards to defend their homes. The oncoming troops had swept past them, but at a tremendous cost. For a whole day the battle had swayed back and forth. Where formerly had bloomed a luxuriant garden or orchard, was now a ploughed field,—ploughed not with farm implements but with shrapnel and high explosive shells. Dotting it here and there, were the little rough wooden crosses that gave the simple details of a man's regimental name, number, and date of death. Not a few of them were in memory of "Unknown Comrades." And once in a while one saw a cross that marked the resting place of the foe. Feeling toward the enemy differed with individuals; but we were all agreed that Johnny Turk was a good, clean, sporty fighter, who generally gave as good as we could send. Therefore, whenever we could we gave him decent burial, we stuck a cross up over him, although he did not believe in what it symbolized, and we took off his identification disk and personal papers. These we handed to our interpreters, who sent them to the neutral consuls at Constantinople; and they communicated through the proper channels with the deceased's various widows.

After a week or so in this district, we moved back again to our old quarters at Anafarta village. Here we took over a block house occupied by the Essex. The Dublins and the Munsters were on our right. The block house was an advanced post that we held in the morning and during the night. Every afternoon we left it for a few hours while the enemy wasted shells on it. A couple of Irish snipers were with us. The first day they were there, our Lieutenant, Mr. Nunns, spent the day with them; that day, he accounted for four Turks. This was the closest we had yet been to them. I stood up beside an Irish sniper and looked through a pair of field glasses to where he pointed out some snipers' dugouts. They were the same dugouts that Cooke, the Irish V.C. man, had shown me. While I was watching, I saw an old Turk sneaking out between his trench and one of the dugouts. He looked old and stooped and had a long whisker that reached almost to his waist and appeared to have difficulty in getting along. All about him were little canvas pockets that contained bombs and about his neck was a long string of small bombs. "Begob," said one of the Dublins, beside me, "'t is the daddy of them all. Get him, my son." I grasped my gun excitedly and aimed; but before I had taken the pressure of the trigger, I heard from a little distance to the right the *staccato* of a machine gun. The result was astonishing. One second, I was looking through my sights at the Turk; the next, he had disappeared, and in his place was the most marvellous combination of all colours of flames I have ever seen. Literally Johnny Turk had gone up in smoke. The Irishman beside me was standing open mouthed.

"Glory be to God," he said, "what does that make you think of?"

"It reminds me," I said, "of a Fourth of July celebration in the States; and I wish," I added heartily, "I was there now."

"It makes me think, my son," said the Irishman, "of the way ould Cooke killed a lot of the sausage-makers over on the other side. He threw a bomb in among tin of 'em and then fired his rifle at it and exploded it. Killed every damn one of 'em, he did. 'T was the same time he got the V.C."

"I suppose," I said, "Cooke's in London now getting his medal from the King. He's through with this Peninsula."

"Thrue for you, my son," said the Irishman, "he's through with this Peninsula, but he's not in London. 'T was just three nights ago

AUSTRALIANS IN THE TRENCHES CONSIDER CLOTHES A SUPERFLUITY

that I went out yonder, and tin yards in front of that dugout I found ould Cooke's body. The Turk got him right through the cap badge and blew the top clean off his head. 'T is just luck. Some has it one way, and some has it another; but whichever way you have it, it don't do you no good to worry over it."

Having delivered himself of this satisfying philosophy, he resumed his survey of the ground in front.

About ten yards outside the block house we were holding, the Turks had, under cover of darkness, almost completed a sap, with the object of surrounding the block house. A detachment of the Dublins with three or four bomb throwers sapped out to the left of the sap the enemy was digging, after a short but exciting engagement, bombed them out of it, and took the sap at the point of the bayonet. They found it occupied by only two Turks, who surrendered. The rest were able to get back to their own trench. We cut the corner off this sap, rounded it off to surround our block house, and occupied it. It brought us to within fifty yards of the enemy firing line. We could hear them talking at night; and in the daytime we could see them walking about their trenches. At this point, they had in their lines a number of animals, chiefly dogs. In addition, they had a brass band that played tuneless, wailing music nearly every night, to the accompaniment of the howling and barking of dogs. Some of the men claimed that the dogs were trained animals who carried food to snipers and who were taught to find the Turkish wounded. This may have been true; but I have always believed that their chief use was to cover the noise of secret operations. This seems likely, for they were able to get their sap almost finished without our hearing them.

The block house we held stood just in the centre of the line that the Fifth Norfolks had charged into early in August, and from which not one man had emerged. The second or third day we occupied it, a detachment of engineers was sent in to make loopholes and prepare it for a stubborn defence. In the wall on the left they made a large loophole. The sentry posted there the first morning saw about twenty feet away the body of a British soldier, partly buried. Two volunteers to bury the body were asked for. Half a dozen offered, although it was broad daylight and the place the body lay in offered no protection.

Before any one could be selected, Art Pratt and young Hayes made the decision by jumping up, taking their picks and shovels, and vaulting over the wall of the block house. They walked out to where the body lay. It had been torn in pieces by a shell the previous afternoon. At first a few bullets tore up little spurts of ground near the two men, but as soon as they reached the body, this stopped. The Turks never fired on burial parties; and men on the Peninsula, wounded by snipers, tell strange stories of dark-skinned visitors who crept up to them after dark, bound up their wounds, gave them water, and helped them to within shouting distance of their own lines, where at daylight the next morning their comrades found them. Once one of our batteries was very near a dressing station when a stray shell, fired at the battery, hit the dressing station. The Turkish observer heliographed over and apologized. That is why we respected the Turk. When we tried to shoot him, he chuckled to himself and sniped us from trees and dugouts; and when we reviled him and threw tins of apricot jam at him, he gave thanks to Allah, and ate the jam. The empty tins he filled with powder and returned to us in the shape of bombs. Only once did he really lose his temper. That was when under his very eyes we deliberately undressed on his beach and disported ourselves in the Aegean Sea. Then he sent over shells that shrieked at us to get out of his ocean. But in his angriest moments he respected the Red Cross and never ill treated our wounded. One chap, an Englishman, was wounded in the head just as he reached the Turkish trench during a charge. The bullet went in the side of his head, ruining both his eyes. He was captured as he toppled over into the trench, was taken to Constantinople, well treated in hospital there, and returned in the first batch of exchanged prisoners. When I met him in Egypt, he had nothing but kind words for the Turks. When the enemy saw the object of the little expedition, they allowed Art and Hayes to proceed unmolested. We watched them dig a grave beside the corpse; and when they had finished, with a shovel they turned the body into it. Before doing it, they searched the man for personal papers and took off his identification disk. These bore the name, "Sergeant Golder, Fifth Norfolk Regiment." That was in the last part of October; and since August 10th not a word had been heard of the missing

Norfolk regiment. To this day, the whole affair remains a mystery. The regiment disappeared as if the ground had swallowed them up. On the King's Sandringham estate, families are still hoping against hope that there may sometime come word that the men are prisoners in Turkey. Neutral consuls in Constantinople have been appealed to, and have taken the matter up with the Turkish Government. The most searching inquiries have elicited nothing new. The answer has always been the same. The Turkish authorities know no more about it than the English. Two hundred and fifty men were given the order to charge into a wood. The only sign that they ever did so, is the little wooden cross that reads:

In Memory of
Sergeant J. Golder
Fifth Norfolk Regiment
Killed in Action

CHAPTER 7

Wounded

The gorgeous tropical sunset had given place to the inky darkness of a Turkish night, when we moved into trenches well up on the side of a hill that overlooked Anafarta plain. Here an advance had been unsuccessful, and the Turks had counter attacked. Half way, the British had dug in hastily, in hard limestone that resisted the pick. No. 8 platoon held six traverses. Four of these were exposed to enfilade fire. About two hundred yards away, at an angle on the left front, a number of snipers had built some dugouts on Caribou Ridge. These they manned with machine guns. From this elevation, they could pour their fire into our trenches. Several attempts had been made to dislodge them; but their machine guns commanded the intervening ground and made an advance impossible. Their first line trench was about two hundred yards in front of us. Thirty or forty yards nearer us they were building a sap that ran parallel with their lines for about five hundred yards. At that point it took a sharp V turn inward toward us. The proximity of the enemy, and the contour of the ground so favourable to them, made it necessary to take extra precautions, especially at night. Each night, at the point where the enemy sap turned toward us, we sent out a listening patrol of two men and a corporal. The fourth night, my turn came. That day it had rained without cessation; and in the early part of the evening I had tried to sleep, but my wet clothes and the pouring rain had made it impossible. I felt rather glad when I was told that at one-thirty I was to go out for two hours on listening patrol. That night we had been issued some rum, and I had been fortunate enough to get a good portion. I decided to reserve it until I went out. About ten o'clock I gave up attempting to sleep, and walked down the trench a little way to where a collection of trees and brush had been laid across the top. Some one, with memories of London's well-known meeting place, had christened it the Marble Arch. I stood under this arch, where the rain did not penetrate, and talked with the corporal of an English regiment who were holding the line on the other side of the Marble Arch. A Sergeant Manson, who had been loaned to us from another platoon, came along and we talked for a while. He had received some chocolate that evening, and the next morning he was going to distribute it among the men. It was in a haversack under his head, he said, and he was going to sleep on it to prevent it from being stolen. About eleven he returned to his place on the firing platform and went to sleep. I was ravenously hungry, and had nothing to eat. I could not find even a biscuit. I did find some bully beef, and ate some of it, washing it down with a swallow of the precious rum from my water bottle. Then I remembered the chocolate under Sergeant Manson's head, and went over to where he was lying. He was breathing heavily in the deep sleep of exhaustion. Quietly I slipped my hand into the haversack, and took out four or five little cubes of chocolate about an inch long. Manson stirred sleepily and murmured, "What do you want?" then turned over and again began breathing regularly. It was now almost time to start for the listening post. So I went along the trench to where I knew young Hayes was sleeping. He had volunteered as one of the men to accompany me, and from D Company I got the second man. My platoon by this time had been reduced to eighteen men, and I was the only non-com. We had to get men from D Company to take turns on the parapet at night, although they were supposed to be resting at the time. Between us and the Turkish sap a small rise covered with short evergreen bushes prevented us from seeing them. To get to this we had to cross about fifty yards of ground with fairly good cover, and another fifty yards of bare ground. Where the bare ground began, a ditch filled with dank, wet grass served as our listening post. A large tree with spreading boughs gave us some shelter. From behind this we could watch the rising ground in front. Any of the enemy attempting an advance had to appear over this rise. Our instructions were to watch this, and report any movement of the enemy, but not to fire. I left young Hayes about half way between this tree and the trench, and the other man and I spread a rubber sheet under the tree and made ourselves as comfortable as possible. The rain was still coming down with a steadiness that promised little hope of stopping. After a little while I became numbed, and decided to move about a little. When I came on the Peninsula, I had no over-coat, but a little time before had secured a very fine gray woollen great-coat from a Turk. It had been at one time the property of a German officer, and was very warm and comfortable, with a large collar and deep thick cuffs. I had worn it about the trench and it had been the subject of much comment. That night I wore it, and over it a raincoat. So that my movements might be less constricted, I took off the raincoat, and left it with the D Company man, who stayed under the tree. It was pitch dark, and I got across the open space to the evergreen-covered rise without being seen. Here I dropped on my stomach and wriggled between wet bushes that pricked my face, up to the top.

It was only about thirty feet, but it took me almost an hour to get up there. By the time I had reached the top it had stopped rain-ing and stars had come out. I crawled laboriously a short distance down the other side of the little hill; I parted the bushes slowly and was preparing to draw myself a little further when I saw something that nearly turned me sick with horror. Almost under my face were the bodies of two men, one a Turk, the other an Englishman. They were both on their sides, and each of them were transfixed with the bayonet of the other. I don't know how long I stayed there. It seemed ages. At last I gathered myself together, and withdrew cautiously, a little to the right. My nerves were so shaken by what I had just seen that I decided to return at once to the man under the tree. When I had gone back about ten feet I was seized with an overwhelming desire to go back and find out to what regiment the dead Englishman belonged. At the moment I turned, my atten-tion was distracted by the noise of men walking not very far to the front. I crawled along cautiously and peered over the top of the rise where I could see the enemy sap. The noise was made by a digging party who were just filing into the sap. For almost an hour I lay there watching them. It gave me a certain satisfaction to aim my rifle at each one in turn and think of the effect of a mere pressure of the trigger. But my orders were not to fire. I was on listening patrol, and we had men out on different working parties, who might be hit in the resulting return fire. At intervals I could hear behind me the report of a rifle, and wondered what fool was shooting from our lines. When I thought it was time to go back I crawled down the hill, and found to my consternation that the moon was full, and the space between the foot of the little rise and the tree was stark white in the moonlight. I had just decided to make a sharp dash across when the firing that I had heard before recommenced. Instead of being from our lines it came from a tree a short distance to the left, at the end of the open space. It was Johnny Turk, cosily ensconced in a tree that overlooked our trench. Whenever he saw a movement he fired. He used some sort of smokeless powder that gave no flash, and it was most fortunate for me that I happened to be at the only angle that he could be seen from. I resumed my wriggling along the edge of the open space to where it ended in thick grass. Through this I crawled until I had come almost to the edge of the ditch in which I had left the other man. But to reach it I had to cross about ten feet of perfectly bare ground that gave no protection. Had the Turk seen me he could have hit me easily. I decided to crawl across slowly, making no noise. I put my head out of the thick grass and with one knee and both hands on the ground poised as a runner does at the start of a race. Against the clear white ground I must have loomed large, for almost at once a bullet whizzed through the top of the little brown woollen cap I was wearing. Just then the D Company man caught sight of me, and raised his gun. "Who goes there?" he shouted. I did some remarkably quick thinking then. I knew that the bullet through my cap had not come from the sniper, and that some one of our men had seen my overcoat and mistaken me for a Turk. I knew the sniper was in the tree, and the D Company's man's challenge would draw his attention to me; also I knew that the Newfoundlander might shoot first and establish my identity afterwards. He was wrong in challenging me, as his instructions were to make no noise. But that was a question that I had to postpone settling. I decided to take a chance on the man in the listening post. I shouted, just loud enough for him to hear me, "Newfoundland, you damn fool, Newfoundland," then tore across the little open space and dived head first into the dank grass beside him. When I had recovered my breath, with a vocabulary inspired by the occasion, I told him, clearly and concisely, what I thought of him. While it may not have been complimentary it was beyond question candid. When I had finished, I sent him back to relieve young Hayes with instructions to send Hayes out to me. In a few minutes Hayes came.

"Do you know, Corporal," he said as he came up beside me, "I almost shot you a few minutes ago. I should have when the other fellow challenged you if you hadn't said 'Newfoundland.' I fired at you once. I saw you go out one way, and when you came back I could just see your Turkish overcoat. 'Here,' says I to myself, 'is Abdul Pasha trying to get the Corporal, and I'll get him.' Instead of that I almost got you."

Whether or not the noise I made caused the sniper to become more cautious I don't know, but I heard no further shots from him from then until the time I was relieved.

The arrival of a relief patrol prevented my replying to young Hayes. I went back to my place in the trench, but try as I might I could not sleep; I twisted from side to side, took off my equipment and cartridge pouches, adjusted blankets and rubber sheet, tried another place on the firing platform; I threw myself down flat in the bottom of the trench. Still I could not get asleep. At last I abandoned the attempt, took from my haversack a few cigarettes, lit one, and on a piece of coarse paper began making a little diagram of the ground I had covered that night, and of the position of the sniper I had been watching. By the time I had completed it daylight had come, and with it the familiar "Stand to." After "Stand to," I crawled under a rubber sheet and snatched a few hours' sleep before breakfast. Just after breakfast, a man from A Company came through the trench, munching some fancy biscuits and carrying in his hand a can of sardines. The German Kaiser could not have created a greater impression. "Where had he got them, and how?" He explained that a canteen had been opened at the beach. Here you could get everything that a real grocery store boasts, and could have it charged on your paybook. "A Company men," he said, "had all given orders through their quarter-master sergeant, and had received them that morning." Then followed a list of mouth-watering delicacies, the very names of which we had almost forgotten. A deputation instantly waited on Mr. Nunns. He knew nothing of the thing, and was incensed that his men had not been allowed to participate in the good things. He deputed me to go down and make inquiries at A Company's lines. I did so, and found that the first man had been perfectly correct. A Company was revelling in sardines, white bread, real butter, dripping from roast beef, and tins of salmon and lobster. If we gave an order that day, I was told, we should get it filled the next. Elated, I returned to B Company's lines with the news. The dove returning to the ark with the olive branch could not have been more welcome. Mr. Nunns fairly beamed satisfaction. A few of the more pessimistic reflected aloud that they might get killed before the things arrived.

Just before nine o'clock I went down to see the cooks about dinner for my section. On my way back I passed a man going down the trench on a stretcher. One of the stretcher bearers told me that he had been hit in the head while picking up rubbish on top of the parapet. He hoped to get him to the dressing station alive. As I came into our own lines another stretcher passed me. The man on this one was sitting up, grinning.

"Hello, Gal," he yelled. "I've stopped a cushy one."

I laughed. "How did it happen?" I asked.

"Picking up rubbish on top of the parapet."

He disappeared around the curve of the trench, delightedly spreading the news that he had stopped a cushy one in the leg. I kept on back to my own traverse, and showed the diagram I had made the night before to Art Pratt. Mr. Nunns had granted us leave to go out that day to try to get the sniper in the tree. Art was delighted at the chance of some variety. While Art and I were making out a list of things we wanted at the canteen, a man in my section came down the trench.

"Corporal Gallishaw," he said, "the Brigade Major passed through the lines a few minutes ago, and he's raising hell at the state of the lines; you've got to go out with five men, picking up rubbish on top of the parapet."

Instantly there came before my eyes the vision of the strangely limp form I had met only a few minutes before that had been hit in the head "picking up rubbish on top of the parapet." But in the army one cannot stop to think of such things long; orders have

Some of the barbed wire entanglements near Seddel Bahr are still in position

to be obeyed. Since coming into the trench we had constructed a dump, but the former occupants of the trench had thrown their refuse on top of the parapet. My job with the five men was to collect this rubbish and put it in our dump. At nine o'clock in the morning we mounted the parapet and began digging. There was no cover for men standing; the low bushes hid men sitting or lying. Every few minutes I gave the men a rest, making them sit in the shelter of the underbrush. The sun was shining brightly; and after the wet spell we had just passed through, the warmth was peculiarly grateful. The news that the canteen had been opened on the beach made most of the men optimistic. With good things to eat in sight life immediately became more bearable. Never since the first day they landed had the men seemed so cheerful. Up there where we were the sun was very welcome, and we took our time over the job. One chap had that morning been given fourteen days' field punishment, because he had left his post for a few seconds the night before. He wanted to get a pipe from his coat pocket, and did not think it worth while to ask any one to relieve him. It was just those few seconds that one of the brigade officers selected to visit our trench. When he saw the post vacant, he waited until the man returned, asked his name, then reported him. Field punishment meant that in addition to his regular duties the man would have to work in every digging party or fatigue detail. I asked him why he had not sent for me, and he told me that it had happened while I was out in the listening patrol. He was not worrying about the punishment, but feared that his parents might hear of it through some one writing home. But after a little while even he caught the spirit of cheerfulness that had spread amongst us at the news of the new canteen. To the average person meals are like the small white spaces in a book that divide the paragraphs; to us they had assumed the proportions of the paragraph themselves. The man who had just got field punishment told me the things he had ordered at the canteen, and we compared notes and made suggestions. The ubiquitous Hayes, working like a beaver with his entrenching tool, threw remarks over his shoulder anent the man who had delayed the information that the canteen had been established, and offered some original and unique suggestions for that individual's punishment.

When we had the rubbish all scraped up in a pile, we took it on shovels to the dump we had dug. To do this we had to walk upright. We had almost finished when the snipers on Caribou Ridge began to bang at us. I jumped to a small depression, and yelled to the men to take cover. They were ahead of me, taking the last shovelful of rubbish to the trench. At the warning to take cover, they separated and dived for the bushes on either side. That is, they all did except Hayes, who either did not hear me or did not know just where to go. I stepped up out of the depression and pointed with outstretched arm to a cluster of underbrush. "Get in there, Hayes!" I yelled. Just then I felt a dull thud in my left shoulder blade, and a sharp pain in the region of my heart. At first I thought that in running for cover one of the men had thrown a pick-axe that hit me. Until I felt the blood trickling down my back like warm water, it did not occur to me that I had been hit. Then came a drowsy, languid sensation, the most enjoyable and pleasant I have ever experienced. It seemed to me that my backbone became like pulp, and I closed up like a concertina. Gradually I felt my knees giving way under me, then my head dropped over on my chest, and down I went. In Egypt I had seen Mohammedans praying with their faces toward Mecca, and as I collapsed I thought that I must look exactly as they did when they bent over and touched their heads to the ground, worshiping the Prophet. Connecting the pain in my chest with the blow in my back, I decided that the bullet had gone in my shoulder, through my left lung, and out through my heart, and I concluded I was done for. I can distinctly remember thinking of myself as some one else. I recollect saying, half regretfully, "Poor old Gal is out of luck this morning," then adding philosophically, "Well, he had a good time while he was alive, anyway." By now things had grown very dim, and I felt everything slipping away from me. I was myself again, but I said to that other self who was lying there, as I thought, dying, "Buck up, old Gal, and die like a sport." Just then I tried to say, "I'm hit." It sounded as if somewhere miles away a faint echo mocked me. I must have succeeded in making myself heard, because immediately I could hear Hayes yell with a frenzied oath, "The Corporal's struck. Can't you see the Corporal's struck?" and heard him curse the Turk who had fired the shot. Almost instantly Hayes was kneeling beside me, trying to find the wound. He was much more excited over it than I.

"Don't you try to bandage it here," I said; "yell for stretcher bearers."

Hayes jumped up, shouting lustily, "Stretcher bearers at the double, stretcher bearers at the double!" then added as an after-thought, "Tell Art Pratt the Corporal's struck."

I was now quite clear headed again and told Hayes to shout for "B Company stretcher bearers." On the Peninsula messages were sent along the trench from man to man. Sometimes when a traverse separated two men, the one receiving the message did not bother to step around, but just shouted the message over. Often it was not heard, and the message stopped right there. One message there was though, that never miscarried, the one that came most frequently, "Stretcher bearers at the double." Unless the bearers from some particular company were specified, all who received the message responded. It was to avoid this that I told Hayes to yell for B Company stretcher bearers. Apparently some one had heard Hayes yell, "Tell Art Pratt the Corporal's struck," because in a few minutes Art was bending over me, talking to me gently. Three other men whom I could not see had come with him; they had risked their lives to come for me under fire. "We must get him out of this," I heard Art say. In that moment of danger his thought was not for himself, but for me. I was able to tell them how to lift me. No women could have been more gentle or tender than those men, in carrying me back to the trench. Although bullets were pattering around, they walked at a snail's pace lest the least hurried movement might jar me and add to my pain. The stretcher bearers had arrived by the time we reached the trench, and were unrolling bandages and getting iodine ready. At first there was some difficulty in getting at the wound. It had bled so freely that the entire back of my coat was a mass of blood. The men who had carried me looked as if they had been wounded, so covered with blood were they. The stretcher bearer's scissors would not work, and Art angrily demanded a sharp knife, which some one produced. The stretcher bearer ripped up my clothing, exposing my shoulder, then began patching up my *right* shoulder. I cursed him in fraternal trench fashion and told him he was working on the wrong shoulder; I knew I had been hit in the *left* shoulder and tried to explain that I had been turned over since I was hit. The stretcher bearer thought I was delirious and continued working away. I thought he was crazy, and told him so. At last Art interrupted to say, "Just look at the other shoulder to satisfy him." They looked, and, as I knew they would, found the hole the bullet had entered. To get at it they turned me over, and I saw that a crowd had gathered around to watch the dressing and make remarks about the amount of blood. I became quite angry at this, and I asked them if they thought it was a nickel show. This caused them all to laugh so heartily that even I joined in. This was when I felt almost certain that I was dying. I can't remember even feeling relieved when they told me that the bullet had not gone through my heart. The pain I felt there when I was first hit was caused by the tearing of the nerves which centred in my heart when the bullet tore across my back from shoulder to shoulder. Never as long as I live shall I forget the solicitude of my comrades that morning. The stretcher bearers found that the roughly constructed trench was too narrow to allow the stretcher to turn, so they put me in a blanket and started away. Meanwhile the word had run along the trench that "Gal had copped it." I did not know until that morning that I had so many friends. A little way down the trench I met Sergeant Manson. He was carrying some sticks of chocolate for distribution among the men. I asked him for a piece. To do so on the Peninsula was like asking for gold, but he put it in my mouth with a smile. Hoddinott and Pike, the stretcher bearers, stopped just where the communication trench began. The doctor had come up. He asked me where I was hit, and I told him. He examined the bandages, and told the stretcher bearers to take me along to the dressing station. Captain Alexander, my company commander, came along, smiled at me, and wished me good-by. Hoddinott asked me if I wanted a cigarette, and when I said, "Yes," placed one in my month and lit it for me. I had never realized until then just how difficult it is to smoke a cigarette without removing it from your mouth. Poor Stenlake, who by this time was worn to a shadow, was in the support trench, waiting with some other sick men, to go to hospital. He came along and said good-by. A Red Cross man gave me a

A British battery at work on the Peninsula

postcard to be sent to some organization that would supply me with comforts while I was in hospital. "You'll eat your Christmas dinner in London, old chap," he said.

We had to go two miles before the stretcher bearers could exchange the blanket for the regular stretcher. The trenches were narrow, and on one side a little ditch had been dug to drain them. The recent wet weather had made the bottom of the trench very slippery, and every few minutes one of the bearers would slide sideways and bring up in the ditch. When he did the blanket swayed with him, and my shoulders struck against the jagged limestone on the sides. To avoid this as much as possible the bearers had to proceed very slowly. Those two miles to me seemed endless. I had now become completely paralyzed, all control of my muscles was gone, and I slipped about in the blanket. Every few yards I would ask Hoddinott, "Is it very much farther?" and every time he would turn around and grin cheerfully, and answer, as one would answer a little child, "Not very much farther now, Gal."

At last we emerged into a large wide communication trench, with the landmarks of which I was familiar. I was suffering severely now, and was beginning to worry over trifles. Suddenly it came to me that I was still a couple of miles from the dressing station, and when we came out of the communication trench on to open ground that had been torn up by shrapnel, I was consumed with fear that at any moment I might be hit by another shell, and might not get aboard the hospital after all, for by this time my mind had centred on getting into a clean bed. A dozen different thoughts chased through my mind. I was grieved to think that in order to get at the wound it had been necessary to cut the fine great-coat that I had so much wanted to take home as a souvenir. I asked Hoddinott what they had done with it, and he told me that part of it was under my head as a pillow, but that it was so besmeared with blood that it would be thrown away as soon as I arrived at the dressing station. From thinking of the great-coat, I remembered that before I went out with the digging party I had taken off my raincoat and left it near my haversack in the trench, and in the pocket of it was the little diagram I had drawn of the position of the sniper I had seen the night before. Again I called for Hoddinott, and again he came, and answered me patiently and gently. "Yes, he would tell Art about the little diagram." Where a fringe of low bushes bordered the pathway at the end of the open space, Hoddinott and Pike turned. For the distance of about a city block they carried the stretcher along a road cut through thick jungle. At the end of it stood a little post from which drooped a white flag with a red cross. It was the end of the first stage for the stretcher bearers. A great wave of loneliness swept over me when I realized that I was to see the last of the men with whom I had gone through so much. I was almost crying at the thought of leaving them there. Somehow or other it did not seem right for me to go. I felt that in some way I was taking an unfair advantage of them. Hoddinott and Pike slipped the straps from their shoulders and lowered the stretcher gently. Under the blanket Hoddinott sought my hand. "Good-by, Gal," he said. "Is there any message I can take back to Art?"

"Yes," I said, "tell him to keep my raincoat."

Since the moment I had been hit, I had been afraid of one thing—that I should break down, and not take my punishment like a man. I was tensely determined that no matter how much I suffered I would not whine or cry. In our regiment it had become a tradition that a man must smile when he was wounded. One thing more than anything else kept me firm in my determination. Art Pratt had walked just behind the blanket until we came to the communication trench. Even then he was loath to leave me. He could not trust himself to speak when I said, "Good-by, Art, old pal." He grasped my hand, and holding it walked along a few feet. Then he dropped my hand gently. There are some things in life that stand out ineffably sweet and satisfying. For me such a one was that last moment of farewell to Art. I had always considered him the most fearless man in a regiment whose name was a byword for reckless courage. Of all men on the Peninsula I valued his opinion most. No recommendation for promotion, no award for valour, not even the coveted V.C., could have been half so sweet as the few words I heard Art say. With eyes shining, he turned to the man beside him and said, almost savagely, "By God, he's a brick."

CHAPTER 8

Homeward Bound

As soon as Hoddinott and Pike had left me, two other stretcher bearers carried me about two hundred yards farther to a rough shelter made of poles laid across supports composed of sandbags. This was the dressing station. On top of the poles, sandbags made it impervious to overhead shelling. On three sides it was closed in, but the side nearest the beach was open. From where my stretcher was placed I could just catch a glimpse of the Aegean Sea and of the ships. Men on stretchers were lined up in rows on the ground. Here and there a man groaned, but most of the men were gazing at the roof, with set faces. Some who were only slightly wounded were sitting up on stretchers while Red Cross men bandaged up their legs or feet. A doctor was working away methodically and rapidly. A little to the right another shelter housed the men who were being sent to hospital with dysentery, enteric, or typhoid. As soon as I was brought in, the doctor came to me. "I'll do this one right away," he said to one of his assistants. The assistant stripped the blanket from me and cut off the portions of the blood-stained shirt still remaining. As he did so, something dropped on the ground. The Red Cross man picked it up.

"Here's the bullet that hit you," he said, putting it beside me on the stretcher. "It dropped out of your shirt. It just got through you and stuck in your shirtsleeve."

"You'd better get him a little bag to keep his things in," said the doctor.

The Red Cross man produced a bag, took my pay book, and everything he found in my pocket, and put them in it, then tied them to the stretcher. By this time I was ready for the doctor to begin work. That doctor knew his business. In a very few minutes he had probed and cut and cleaned the wound, and adjusted a new bandage. The bleeding had stopped by this time. He asked me the circumstances of being hit. He told me to grip his hand and squeeze. I tried it with my right hand but could do nothing; then I tried the left hand and succeeded a little better. The doctor looked grave when I failed to grip with my right hand, but brightened a little when I gripped with my left. All the time he talked to me genially. That did me nearly as much good as the surgical attention he gave me. He was a Canadian, he told me. At the outbreak of the war he had been taking post-graduate courses at Cambridge University in England. The University sent several hospital units to the front, and he had come with this one. He knew Canada and the States pretty thoroughly.

"Where do you come from?" he asked me.

"Newfoundland," I told him. "But I live in the United States."

"What part?" he asked.

"Cambridge, Massachusetts," I told him.

"Oh," he said, "that's where Harvard University is."

"Yes," I said, "I was a student there when I enlisted."

The doctor called to a couple of the Red Cross men. "Here's a chap from Harvard University in Cambridge, over in the United States." The two Red Cross men came and told me they were students at Cambridge. They talked to me for quite a little while. Before they left me to attend to some more wounded, they made me promise to ask to be sent to Cambridge, England, to hospital. The University had established a very large and thoroughly equipped hospital there. All I had to do, they said, was tell the people that I had been a student at the other Cambridge, and I should be an honoured guest. They persisted in calling Harvard, Cambridge, and when they went away said that they were overjoyed to have seen a man from the sister university.

The doctor came back in a few minutes.

"How are you feeling now?" he said.

"I feel pretty well now," I answered, "but it's very close in here with all these wounded men, and the place smells of chloroform. Can't I be moved outside?"

"I'll move you outside if you say so," said the doctor, "but you're

107

taking a chance. Occasionally a stray shell comes over this way. The Turks are trying to locate a battery close to this place. Sometimes a shell bursts prematurely, and drops around here."

On the Peninsula, officers who gave men leave to go on dangerous missions salved their consciences by first warning the men that in doing it "they were taking a chance." The caution had come to mean nothing.

"All right, doctor," I said. "I'll take a chance."

Two stretcher bearers came, and lifted me outside the shelter, where the wind blew, fresh and invigorating. Just as they turned, I heard the old familiar shriek that signalled the coming of a shell. It burst almost overhead. Most of the missiles it contained dropped on the other side of the shelter, but a few tiny pieces flew in my direction. Three of them hit me in the right arm, a fourth landed in my leg.

"Is anybody hit?" yelled a Red Cross man, whose accent proclaimed him as an inhabitant of the country north of the Clyde.

"I've got a couple of splinters," I said.

I was lifted inside quickly. The Scotchman who put on some bandages on the little cuts looked at me accusingly.

"Ye were warned, before ye went," he said. "Ye desairved it. But then," he added, "ye might hae got it worse. Ye're lucky ye did not get it in the guts."

After a little while my arms and back began to ache violently. Two Red Cross men came along and moved me to another shelter similar to the first. This was the clearing station. From here motor ambulances carried the wounded to the shore. I knew from the burring speech of the big sergeant in charge that he hailed from Scotland. I asked him where he came from, and he told me that he came from Inverness.

"Our regiment trained near there for a while," I said. "They garrisoned Fort George."

"Ye'll no' be meanin' the Seaforth Highlanders, laddie," said he.

"No," I said, "we're Newfoundlanders, the First Newfoundland Regiment."

"Oh, I ken ye well, noo," he said, gloomily. "Ye're a bad lot; it took six policemen to arrest one o' your mob. On the Peninsula they call ye the Never Failing Little Darlings." After that he thawed quite a little. "I'll look at your wound noo, laddie," he said, after a few minutes. "Ye're awfu' light, laddie," he said as he raised me. "Puir laddie," he added, pityingly. "Puir laddie. Ye're stairved. I'll get ye Queen Mary's ration."

"What's Queen Mary's ration?" I asked.

"'T's Queen Mary's gift to the wounded. I'll get it for ye right away." He went outside the clearing station and returned in a few minutes with a cup of warm malted milk. "'T will help ye some till ye get aboard the hospital ship. Here's the ambulance noo."

A fleet of motor ambulances swayed over the uneven ground and rolled up close to the clearing station. The drivers and helpers began loading the stretchers aboard and one by one started away. Before I was put into one, the big Scotchman took a large syringe and injected a strong dose of *morphia* into my chest.

"Ye'll find it hard," he said, "bumping over the hill, but ye'll soon be all right and comfortable."

"Tell me," I said, "shall I get into a real bed on the ship?"

He laughed. "Sure ye will, laddie. The best bed ye've had since ye've been in the airmy. Good luck to ye, laddie."

Each of the motor ambulances carried four men, two above and two below. I was put on top, and the door flap pulled over. We jolted and pitched and swayed. Once we turned short and skid-ded at a curve. I knew just the very place, although it was dark in the ambulance. I had gone over the road often with ration parties. Fortunately the *morphia* was beginning to take effect, and dulled the pain to some extent. At last the ambulance stopped, somebody pulled the curtain back, and we were lifted out. We were on West Beach. A pier ran out into the sea. A man-o'-war launch towing a string of boats glided in near enough to let her first boat come close to the pier. The breeze was quite fresh, and made me shiver. The stretchers were laid across the boats, close to each other. Soon all the boats were filled. I could see the man on the stretcher to the right of me, but the one on the other side I could not see. I tried to turn my head but could not. The eyes of the man next me were large with pain. I smiled at him, but instead of smiling back at me, his lip curled resentfully, and he turned over on his side so that he could face away from me. As he did, the blanket slipped from his shoulder, and I saw on his shoulder strap the star of a second lieutenant. I had committed the unpardonable sin. I had smiled at an officer as if I had been an equal, forgetting that he was not made of common clay. Once after that, when he turned his head, his eyes met mine disdainfully. That time I did not smile. I have often laughed at the incident since, but there on that boat I was boiling with rage. Not a word had passed between us, but his expression in turning away had been eloquent. I cursed him and the system that produced him, and swore that never again would I put on a uniform. Gradually I calmed down; the *morphia* had got in its work. In a little while I had sunk into a comatose condition. I remember, in a hazy sort of way, being taken aboard a large lighter. There were tiers of stretchers on both sides. This time I was in the lower tier, and was wondering how soon the man above me would fall on me. At last I went to sleep. When I awoke, I was alone and in mid-air. All about me was black. By that time I was completely paralyzed from the waist up. I could see only directly above my head. It was night, and the sky was dotted with twinkling stars. I could feel no movement, but the stars came slowly nearer and nearer. "What was I doing here in mid-air?" Subconsciously I thought of the body of Mohammed, suspended between earth and heaven. Now I felt I had hit on the answer. I was going to heaven, and the thought was very comforting. Suddenly the stars stopped, and after a pause began receding. A face appeared above me, then the head and shoulders of a man dressed in the uniform of a naval officer. This suggested something else to me. The officers of the Flying Corps wear naval uniforms. I decided that while I was asleep I had been transferred to the Flying Corps.

"Hello, old chap," said the naval officer. "Do you know where you are?"

"No," I said. "Am I going to heaven, or have I joined the Flying Corps?"

"No," said the officer. "You're on the stretcher being hoisted aboard the hospital ship."

Two big, strapping, bronzed sailors approached and lifted the stretcher on to an elevator; they stepped on and the elevator descended. We stopped at the end of a short white-walled passageway, lighted by electricity. The sailors grasped the stretcher as lightly as if it had been empty, walked along to the end of the passageway into a ward. It had formerly been a dining saloon. Large square windows looked out upon the sea, everything was white and clean and orderly. After the dirt and filth of the Peninsula it was like a beautiful dream. The sailors lifted me gently into a bed and stood there waiting for orders from the nurse. As I looked at them I thought of our boys standing in the trenches during a bombardment and yelling, "Come on, the navy," and I murmured, "Come on, the navy;" and then when I looked at the calm, self-possessed, capable-looking nursing sister, moving about amongst the wounded, I said, and never had it meant so much to me, "Good old Britain."

The string of boats in which I had come was the batch that filled the quota of the patients of the hospital ship. In about half an hour she began to move. An orderly came around with meals. The doctor came in after a little while and began examining the patients. From some part of the ship not far from where I was came the sound of voices singing hymns. It was the last touch needed to emphasize the difference between the hospital ship and the Peninsula. Sunday evening on the Peninsula had meant no more than any other. The ship moved along so quietly that she seemed scarcely to stir. The doctor and the nurse worked noiselessly; over everything hung the spirit of Sabbath calm. Gallipoli might have been as far away as Mars.

It must have been about nine o'clock when an orderly came around and turned out all the lights except a reading lamp over the desk where the night sister sat. All that night I could not sleep. About midnight the night sister gave me a sleeping draught, but it did no good. I was suffering the most intense pain, but I was so glad to be away from the dirt of the trenches that I felt nothing else counted. The next day I was a great deal weaker, and could scarcely talk. When the doctor came around to dress my wounds, I could only smile at him. All that day the sister came to my bed at frequent intervals. I was too weak then to eat. Two or three times she gave me some sort of broth through a little feeding bowl. In the evening I had sunk into apathy. The sister sent for the doctor. He came, felt my pulse, took my temperature, then turned and whispered to the sister. She called an orderly, and I heard her say, "Bring the screens for this man." The orderly went away and in a few minutes returned with two screens large enough to entirely conceal my

With the French at Seddel Bahr

bed. When the screens had been put in position, the sister came in, wiped my mouth and forehead, and went away. On the other side of the screen I heard her speaking softly to the doctor. The whole thing seemed to me something entirely apart from me. I felt that I was watching a scene in a play, and that I found it of little interest. After about an hour the doctor and the sister came in again.

"Feeling all right, old man?" said the doctor.

"Yes," I said. "Fine."

"Sister," said the doctor, "give this man anything he wants."

The sister bent over me. She was a woman between thirty and thirty-five, of the type that inspires confidence; every word and movement reflected poise, and there was a calmness and serenity about her that you knew she could have acquired only as a result of having seen and eased much human suffering.

"If there is anything you would care to have, please ask for it, and if it is at all possible we will get it for you," she said, in a softly modulated voice, with the slightest suspicion of a drawl; it was the voice of a cultivated English-woman; after the Peninsula, a woman's voice was like a tonic.

"Yes," I said, "I want chicken and wine."

I had not the slightest desire for chicken and wine just then, but I felt that I had to ask for something, and the best I could think of was chicken and wine. She smiled at me, went away, and in about fifteen minutes she returned with a little tray. She had brought the chicken and wine. She had minced up the chicken, and she fed me little pieces of it with a spoon. In a little cup with a spout she had the wine. When I had eaten a little of the chicken, she put the spout between my lips; I had expected some port wine, but when I tasted, it was champagne. I drank it to the very last drop.

"How do you feel now?" said the sister.

"Never felt better," I answered.

"That's very nice," she said. "I hope you'll get to sleep soon."

Then she went away, and in a few minutes the night sister came on. She peeped in at me, smiled, and went away. All that night I looked up at a tiny spot on the ceiling. In the board directly above my eyes, there was a curious knot. A little flaw ran across the centre of it. It reminded me of a postman carrying his bag of letters. It seemed to me that night that I could stand the pain no longer. My back seemed to be tearing apart, as if a man was pulling on each shoulder, trying to separate them from the spine. I tried to jump up from the bed but could not move a muscle. I felt that it would be better to tear my back apart myself at once and have it over, but when I tried to move my arms I found them useless. It must have been well into the morning when the night sister came around again. The doctor was with her. He had a large syringe in his hand. He said nothing. Neither did I. I closed my eyes. I wanted to be alone. I felt him open my shirt at the neck and rub some liquid on my chest. I opened my eyes. He was putting the needle of the long-syringe into my chest where he had rubbed it with iodine. The skin was leathery and at first the needle would not penetrate. At last it went in with a rush. It seemed at least a foot long. He rubbed another spot, and plunged the needle in a second time. "We've got to get him asleep," he said to the night sister. "If he's not asleep in an hour, call me again." Very soon a drowsiness crept over me. Nothing seemed to matter. I wanted to rest. In a short time I was asleep. When I woke, it was broad daylight. The day sister was standing by my bed, smiling. She turned around and beckoned to some one. The doctor came close to the bed, felt my pulse, took my temperature again, and smiled. "Quite all right, sister," he said.

An orderly came in, lifted me up in bed, washed my face and hands, and brought in a tray with chicken. There was the same little feeding cup. This time it had port wine in it. The orderly propped me up in bed, putting cushions carefully behind my back and shoulders. The sister and the doctor superintended while he was doing it. Lifting a wounded man is a science. An unskilful person, no matter how well intentioned, may sometimes do incalculable damage. Putting a strain on the wrong muscle may undo the work of the doctor. I could see out one of the large windows now, and I noticed that we were passing a good many ships, mostly vessels of war. They seemed to increase in number every few minutes; and by the time I had finished breakfast, we were in the midst of a forest of funnels and rigging. Soon the engines stopped. When the doctor came around to dress my back, I asked him where we were.

"We're in Alexandria, now," he said. "In an hour's time we'll

114

have unloaded. You're the last patient to be dressed. We're doing you last so that you won't have so long to wait before the bandages are changed."

"Doctor," I asked, "how long will it be before this wound gets better?"

"I don't know," he said. "It's impossible to tell until you've been X-rayed. Last night we were certain you were dying, but this morning you are perfectly normal."

In a short time the ward filled with men from the shore, landing officers, orderlies with messages, sergeants in charge of ambulance corps, and an army of stretcher bearers. The orderlies of the hospital ship began putting out the kits of the wounded at the foot of their beds. The disembarkation began as soon as the doctor had completed his dressing. I was propped up in bed, and could see a long line of motor ambulances on the pier. The less seriously wounded cases were taken off first. The sister told me that these were going by train to Cairo. Those who could not stand the train journey were going to different hospitals in Alexandria. I was to go to Alexandria, she said. A middle-aged man passed us on a stretcher. He was hit in the leg, and sat on the stretcher, smiling contentedly, and looking about him interestedly. When he saw the sister, his eyes lighted up.

"Good-by, sister," he shouted. "I'll see you again, the next time I'm wounded."

The sister returned his good-by. Then she turned to me, and said: "That man was on the hospital train that left Antwerp the day the Germans shelled it in 1914. When he came in the other night I didn't recognize him, but he remembered me."

While I waited for my turn the sister told me that she had been in the first batch of nurses to cross the Channel at the beginning of the war. She had been in the hospitals in Belgium that were shelled by the Germans. At eight o'clock in the morning she had left Antwerp on the last hospital train, and at nine o'clock the Germans occupied the town. She had been on different hospital ships and trains ever since. Once only had she had a rest. That was some time in the summer of 1915. She expected a week off in London at Christmas, when the ship she was now attached to laid up for repairs. The boat I was on, she said, carried ordinarily seven hun-

WHERE TROOPS LANDED IN DARDANELLES SHOWING FORT SED-NE-BEHI BATTERED TO PIECES BY ALLIED FLEET

dred and fifty wounded. At present she carried nine hundred. They generally arrived in Suvla Bay in the morning, and left that night, filled with wounded. At the time of the first landing at Anzac an hour after the assault began they left with twelve hundred wounded Australians. The sisters were sent out from a central depot in England, and went to the various fronts. When the stretcher bearers came to take me away, the sister gathered up my belongings in a little bag, tied it to the stretcher, put a pillow under my head, and nodded a bright good-by.

The stretcher bearers, two stalwart Australians, took me to the elevator, across the deck, and out onto the pier. It was now getting toward evening. A lady stopped the stretcher between the pier and the ambulance, and handed one of the bearers a little white packet containing a towel, soap, tooth-brush and tooth-powder. Without waiting to be thanked she went on to intercept another stretcher. The stretcher bearer put the package under my pillow. "Ready, Bill," said one of the bearers with the nasal twang of the Bushman. "Lift away," said Bill, and they lifted the stretcher up on the top tier of the ambulance wagon, without stepping up from the ground. They did it with the same motion as when two men swing a bag of grain. But it was not in the least uncomfortable for me. These Australian stretcher bearers who meet the incoming hospital ships are amazingly strong. There is an easy gracefulness in the way they swing along with a stretcher that makes you trust them. I was the last man to go in that ambulance wagon, and in a few minutes we were whirling smoothly along good roads amid the familiar smells of Egyptian bazaars. This ambulance drive was a good deal different from the one on the Peninsula just after I had been wounded. After about half an hour the ambulance swerved off the smooth asphalt road onto a gravel road, slowed down, and ran into a yard. The Australians reappeared, opened the flaps, and began unloading. We were in the square of a large hospital. All around us were buildings. A fine-looking, bronzed man, with the uniform of a colonel, was directing some Sikhs who were carrying the stretchers from the ambulances into the different buildings. All the stretchers were lying on the ground in a long row. As soon as each one was inspected by the colonel, he told the stretcher bearers where to take it. When he came to mine, he said, "Dangerously wounded, Ward three." Then, to the stretcher bearers, "Careful, very careful."

Ward three was a long ward with stone floor and plaster walls; it contained about fifty beds. More than half of the beds had little "cradles" at the foot; when I came to know hospitals, I learned that these were to prevent the bedclothes from irritating wounded legs. In a few minutes a doctor came around, gave orders, and the night sister began bandaging up the wounds of the men who had come in. The sister who arranged my bandages was Scotch, and the burr of her speech was pleasant in my ears. She came back about ten o'clock and gave me a sleeping potion. The change from the hospital ship must have been too much excitement for me, because I could not get asleep that night. But I did not feel as I had felt on the hospital ship. I have very seldom experienced such joy as I did that night when I found that I could move my head. I did it very slowly, and with great pain, and rested a long time before I tried to turn it back again. The door was right opposite my bed. I could see the sand shining white in the moonlight in the square, and right ahead of me a large marquee where, I found out later, some of the convalescent men slept. A man about four beds away from mine was dying. When I had first come in he had been groaning at intervals, but now he was silent. About one or two o'clock an orderly came running softly in rubber-soled shoes to tell the sister that the man had died. Half an hour later two men with a particularly long stretcher, appeared in the ward. They stepped quietly, trying not to disturb the sleepers. I saw them walk along to the bed of the dead man, and go in behind the screen. After a little while the ward orderly moved the screens back, and the stretcher bearers reappeared. Over the burden on the stretcher was draped a Union Jack. Often after that while I was in Ward three I saw the same soft-stepping men come in at night and depart silently with the flag-draped stretcher. Many of the wounded left the ward in that way, but their places were soon filled by incoming wounded. The first morning I was in Ward three the doctor ordered me to be X-rayed. The X-ray apparatus was in another building. To get to it I had to pass through the square. The sun was too hot in the morning for us to cross the square. We therefore skirted it under the shade of the long portico that runs along the outside of nearly all buildings in Egypt. In beds outside the building were men with dysentery. At the corner of the square a plank gangway led to the quarters of the enteric patients. Just before I reached the X-ray room, a man hailed me from one of the beds. It was Tom Smythe, a boy I had known since I was able to walk. All the time I had been on the Peninsula I had not seen him, nor had I heard any news of him. On the way back from the X-ray room, the stretcher bearers stopped near his bed while I talked with him. He had been in the hospital about two weeks, he said, and hoped to get to England on the next boat. He promised to come to see me in my ward as soon as he was allowed up. The next day he came, although he was not supposed to be up, and brought with him a chap named Varney. Varney had been in the section next mine at Stob's Camp in Scotland, he told me. Smythe and Varney vied with each other after that in trying to make me comfortable. To me that has always been the most remarkable thing about our regiment: their loyalty to a comrade in trouble. I have known Newfoundlanders to fight with each other, using every weapon from profanity to tent mallets while in camp; on the Peninsula I have seen these same men carrying each other's packs, digging dugouts, and taking the other man's fatigue work. Varney was very much distressed to see the condition I was in. He knew I was fond of reading, and searched all over the place for books and magazines. Once he brought me three American magazines, one *Saturday Evening Post* and two *Munsey's*. They were nearly two years old, but I read them as eagerly as if they had just been published.

During the six weeks I was in hospital in Alexandria, I improved wonderfully. The doctor in charge of the ward took a special interest in my progress, and seemed to pride himself on having handled the case successfully. Every day or so he brought in a doctor from some other ward to show him my wounds and the X-ray plates. He was very careful and tried in dressing to cause me as little pain as possible. "Poor old chap," he would say, when he saw me wince, "poor old chap." I think there was a great deal of psychology in my getting well. In this Twenty-first General Hospital nothing was omitted that could make one comfortable. Every morning an orderly washed me. The orderlies were all very considerate, except one. He did not last very long in our ward. He began washing the patients at four o'clock in the morning. He always made me think of a hostler washing a carriage. When he had washed my arms he always let them drop in a way that reminded me of the shafts of a wagon. He was soon replaced by a chap who did not begin his work until seven. At eight we had breakfast: fruit, cereal, and eggs. At eleven we had soda water and crackers or sweet biscuits. At one came dinner: soup, chicken, and vegetables, half a chicken to each man, with a dessert of pudding or custard. At four we had tea, with fish, and at eight came supper: cocoa and bread and butter, with jelly. In the morning visitors came in and brought us the daily papers. Sisters of the V.A.D.—Voluntary Aid Detachment—came in each afternoon to relieve the regular nursing sisters. They were mostly Englishwomen resident in Egypt. Most of their men folks were at one of the fronts. They read to the men who could not hold books in their hands, talked to us cheerfully, and wrote letters for us. Some of them brought us little delicacies: grapes and chocolate. Men in hospital have no money. Any money they have is taken away when they arrive and refunded when they leave. Like most of the rules in the army to-day, this was made for the old regulars. When the regulars felt they needed a rest they went into hospital; the only way they could be stopped was to keep all their money away from them. To-day two million men suffer as a result. Ever since the day I left the Peninsula I had wanted chocolate. But I had no money, and for a long time I had to go without it. At last young Varney got me some. He had gone errands for a wounded Australian, who had been given some money from outside, and the Australian had given him some; he could hardly wait to get to me with it.

As soon as a man was sufficiently recovered to travel, he was sent to England. New men were always coming in to take the places of the old. A lot of them were Australians. I kept asking them all as they came in if they could tell me anything of my friend White George. Of course a nickname is very little to go on. A man who was White George in one part of the trench might be Queensland Harry in another. All I knew about him was that he was in the Fifteenth Battalion, and that he had a beard. At last a chap did come in one evening from the Fifteenth Battalion. I was in bed at the time, and could not get a chance to ask him about White George. The next day the poor chap was writhing and screaming in the terrible spasms of tetanus, and for two days the screens were around his bed. On the third day he was better. As soon as Varney came in, he wheeled me up to the Australian's bed. I asked him what was the matter with him, and he told me that he had a flesh wound in the head that didn't bother him, but that his left leg was off at the knee.

"Are you from the Fifteenth Battalion?" I asked.

"Yes," he said.

"Do you know a chap in that battalion," I said, "that they call White George?"

The wounded Australian looked at me in a quizzical way. Then he drawled slowly, "Well, I think I do. Why, damn it, man, I'm White George."

Then he recognized me. "Why, it's the Newfoundland Corporal. Hello, Corporal. You're just the man I wanted to see," he said. "I stood on that bomb all right, and got away with it—once. When I tried it a second time, I put the bomb on the firing platform, and when I stepped on it, my head was over the parapet; Johnny Turk got me in the head, and the bomb did the rest."

"Don't you wish now you hadn't tried the experiment?" I said.

"No," said White George, "I feel perfectly satisfied."

"By the way," I said, as I was leaving him, "why do they call you White George? Your hair is dark."

"My real name," he said, "is George White, but on the regimental roll it reads 'White, George.'"

CHAPTER 9

"Feenish"

It must have been about the sixth week that I was in Egypt that one of the Australians came over to my bed and told me that my name was on the list of men to go to England by the next boat. I was allowed up for two hours in the afternoon; and when I got up I looked at the list, and found my name there. An orderly from the stores came in and asked me for a list of clothing I needed. He came back in about an hour with a complete uniform and kit. The sister told me that I was to go to England the next morning. At ten o'clock the next day I was taken out to the little clearing station in the square, and put in with a lot of other men on stretchers. An officer came around and inspected our kits. A little later a sergeant from the pay office gave each man an advance of twelve shillings. After that the loading began. A line of about twenty ambulances filed out of the yard and through the malodorous byways of Alexandria to the waterfront. Here we were put aboard the hospital ship *Rewa*, an old rocky tub that had been an Indian troopship before the war. I learned this from an old English regular in the stretcher next me. He had seen her often before, and had made a trip from England to India in her once. The *Rewa* was so full of men that the latest arrivals had to go on deck in hammocks. The thought of a trip across the Bay of Biscay as deck passenger on the *Rewa* was not very attractive, but our fears on this point were soon allayed by one of the ship's officers. We were not going to England on the *Rewa*, he said. We were going to Lemnos Island, and in Mudros Bay we should tranship into the *Aquitania*. When we had cleared Alexandria Harbour, the wind had freshened considerably. All that night and the next day we pitched and rolled heavily. The second night, when we had expected to reach Mudros Bay, we were still twenty-four hours away from it. Canvas sheets had to be rigged above the bulwarks to prevent the spray from drenching the men in the stretchers on deck. The next day a good many men were sea sick, and it was not till the next evening that the storm abated. Even then it was too rough to get close to the big ship. We did try to get near her once, and succeeded in getting one hawser fast, but the wind and tide drove us so hard against her, that the captain of the *Aquitania* would take no more risks and ordered us off. We had to lay to all that evening, and the next morning. At noon the wind died down enough to begin the trans-shipment from the smaller ships. We waited while seven other hospital ships transferred their human freight, and then moved up near enough to put gangways between the two boats. The change was effected very expeditiously. We were soon transferred, and settled in our new quarters. I was in a ward with some Australian troops on the top deck. Board petitions had been run up from it to the promenade deck, making a long bright, well ventilated corridor. There was only one drawback on the *Aquitania*. The sister in charge of our ward did not like Colonials, and made it pretty plain. She was rather a superior person who did not like to dress wounds. We were to make two stops before we arrived in England, I was told; one at Salonika to take on some sick, the other at Naples for coal. The Salonika stop took place at night. We did not go into the harbour; probably it was not deep enough for the *Aquitania*. The sick were taken aboard outside. We came to Naples early one fine Sunday morning. As we went into the harbour, I could see through the window Mt. Vesuvius, smoking steadily. We were in Naples at the same time as the big *Olympic*, and the *Mauretania*, the sister ship of the *Lusitania*. It was the time that the Germans had protested that the British hospital ships carried troops to the Dardanelles on the return trip. The neutral consuls in Naples went aboard the *Olympic* and *Mauretania* that Sunday and investigated. The charge, of course, was unfounded. An Italian general and his staff came aboard our ship and were shown around the wards. He was a dapper little man, who gesticulated vehemently and bowed to all the sisters. The sister who did not like Colonials was speaking to him when he came through our ward. She was trying to impress him with the excellent treatment our wounded received. She pointed out each man to him, in the same way a keeper does at the zoological gardens.

"They get this every evening," she said, indicating the supper we were eating. "And what is this?" she said, looking at some apricot jam on a saucer on my bed.

"Apricot jam, sister," I said, then added sweetly, in my best society fashion, "We get it every evening." I might have told her that I had had it not only every evening, but every noon and morning while I was on the Peninsula.

"And what is this?" she said, pointing to the cup in my hand. "Is it tea or cocoa?"

"It's tea," I said. "We get it every evening,—just as if we were human beings, and not Colonials." After that I think she liked Colonials even less.

The Bay of Biscay was just a little rough when we went through it, but it did not affect the *Aquitania* very much.

When the word went around on the day that land had been sighted, every man that could hobble went on deck to get a first glimpse of England. We could not see very far because of the thick mist of an English December. About ten o'clock we were at the entrance to Southampton, but the tide was out, or the chief engineer was out, so we could not go up until that evening. That last day was a tedious one. Every one was eager to get ashore. To most of the men, England was home; and after the trenches and the hospitals, home meant much.

As soon as we landed, a train took us to a place near London. It was twenty-five miles from the hospital that was our destination. Here we were met by automobiles that took us to the hospital for Newfoundlanders at Wandsworth Common, London. There were only half a dozen of us from Newfoundland. At first the doctor on the *Aquitania* persisted in calling us Canadians, and wanted to send us to Walton-on-Thames. It took us two hours to convince him that Newfoundland had no connection with Canada. Two automobiles were enough for our little party. The man who drove me in told me that he had come a hundred miles to do it. All the automobiles that met the hospital trains were loaned by people who wanted to do whatever they could to help the cause. He was a dairy farmer, he said, and gave me uninteresting statistical information about cows and the amount of milk he sold in London each day. But apart from that, I enjoyed the smooth drive over the faultless roads.

The Third London hospital at Wandsworth Common is a military hospital; and although the discipline is strict, everything possible is done for the comfort of the patients. Concerts are given every few evenings; almost every afternoon people send around automobiles to take the wounded men for a drive. Twice a week visitors come in for three hours in the afternoon. At Wandsworth I stayed only a very few days. Two days before Christmas I was sent to Esher to the convalescent home run by the V.A.D. Sisters. Nobody at this hospital received any remuneration. Esher is in Surrey, not many miles from London. Even in the winter the weather was pleasant. Here we had a great deal of liberty, being allowed out all day until six at night. Only thirty men were in Esher at one time. The hospital contained a piano, victrola, pool table, and materials for playing all sorts of games. At Esher one felt like an individual, and not like a cog in a machine. Paddy Walsh, the corporal, who had hesitated so long about leaving me on the Peninsula, was at Esher when I arrived. He was almost well now, he told me, and was looking forward to a furlough. After his furlough he was going back, he said, in the first draft. "No forming fours for me, around Scotland," said Walsh, "drilling a bunch of rookies. I want to get back with the boys."

After two weeks, Esher closed for repairs. We all went back to the hospital at Wandsworth. News had just come of the evacuation of the Peninsula. In the ward I was sent to were half a dozen of our boys. I asked them what was the trouble, and they told me frozen feet. "Frozen feet," I said, "in Gallipoli? You're joking."

They assured me that they were not and referred me to their case sheets that hung beside the beds. Shortly before the evacuation a storm had swept over the Peninsula. First it had rained for two days, the third day it snowed, and the next it froze. A torrent of water had poured down the mountain side, flooding the trenches, and carrying with it blankets, equipments, rifles, portions of the parapet, and the dead bodies of men who had been drowned while they were sleeping. The men who were left had to forsake their trenches and go above ground. Turks and British alike suffered. The last day of the storm, while some of our men were waiting on the beach to be taken to the hospital ship, they told me they saw the bodies of at least two thousand men, frozen to death. Our regiment stood it perhaps better than any of the others. It was the sort of climate they were accustomed to. The Australians suffered tremendously. I met one man who had been on the Peninsula during the evacuation. They had got away with the loss of two men killed and one wounded for the entire British force. The papers that day said that the Turks claimed to have driven the entire British army into the sea, and to have gained an immense amount of booty. The booty gained, our men said, was bully beef and biscuits. Far from being driven into the sea, the British got off in two hours without the Turks suspecting at all; and it was not till the second day after that the Turks really found out. It had taken a great deal of ingenuity to devise a scheme that would let the evacuation take place secretly. The distance from the shore was about four miles. As soon as the troops knew they were to leave, they ripped up the sand bags on the parapets, and broke the glass in the periscopes, so they would be useless to the enemy. Then they attached the broken periscopes to the parapets, so that the Turks looking over would see the periscopes above the trench, just as they would any ordinary day at the front. Only one problem remained unsolved. As soon as the Turks heard the firing cease entirely, they would think something was not as it should be. If they began to investigate before the troops got away, it might mean annihilation. At first it was planned to leave a small party scattered through the trenches, but this meant that they would have to be sacrificed in order to allow their comrades to escape. An Australian devised a scheme. He took a number of rifles, placed them at different points along the parapets, and lashed them to it. In each one he put a cartridge. From the trigger he suspended a bully beef tin, weighted with sand. This was not quite heavy enough to pull the trigger. On top of the rifle he placed another tin, filled with water, and pierced a small hole in the bottom of it. After a while the water, dripping slowly from the top tin, made the lower one heavy enough to pull the trigger. Some of the tins were heavier than the others, and the rifles did not all go off at once. As soon as things were ready, the troops moved off silently, "Just as if they were going into dugouts," Art Pratt wrote me. They got aboard the warships waiting for them in the bay, and went to Mudros and Imbros. The evacuation was facilitated by the fact that the Salt Lake that had been dried up when I was there was swollen high by the rain of the previous weeks. All that night the firing continued at intervals, and kept up all through the next day. The Turks, taking the usual cautious survey of the enemy trenches, saw, as they did every other day, periscopes sticking up over the parapets and heard the ordinary reports of rifle fire; to them it looked like what the official reports call a "quiet day on the Eastern front."

One other item of news I received that pleased me very greatly. Art Pratt had taken my place as corporal of the section, and had sent me word that he had got the sniper who shot me.

After I had been back in the Wandsworth Common hospital a few days, I was "boarded." That is, I was sent up to be examined by a board of doctors. They found me "unfit for further service," and I was sent to my depot in Scotland for disposal. The next day I was given all my back pay and took the train for Ayr, Scotland. There I was given my discharge "in consequence of wounds received in action in Gallipoli." Major Whitaker, the officer in charge, paused and looked at me, while he was signing the discharge paper.

"I imagine," he said, "you feel rather sorry that you caught that train, Corporal."

"What train is that, sir?" I said.

"The one at Aldershot," he answered, as he completed his signature. I smiled noncommittally, but did not answer him.

Looking back now it seems to me that catching that train is one thing I have never regretted. I was convinced of it that day in Ayr. For a few weeks past convalescents of the First Battalion had been dribbling into Ayr. You could tell them by their wan, fever-wasted faces, and by the little ribbons of claret and white that they wore on the sleeves of their coats, the claret and white that marked them as the "service battalion." And there was in their faces, too, the calm, confident look of men who had hobnobbed with death, and had come away unafraid. Every one of them had the same tale. "We're tired of the depot already. They're a new bunch here, and we want to get back with the crowd we know." There was no talk of patriotism, or duty; all this had given place to the pride of local achievement. To those men, my little claret and white ribbon was all the introduction I needed. I was a member of the First Battalion. As I hobbled along the main street of Ayr, a crowd of them bore down on me. A heterogeneous bunch they were, bored to death with the quietness of the Scottish town, shouting boisterous greetings long before they reached me. The lot of us took dinner together and afterwards went in a body to the theatre. The theatre proprietor refused unconditionally to take any money from us. We were "returned wounded," and the best seats in the house were ours. Four or five of our party had just returned from Edinburgh, where they had spent their furloughs. They had been received royally. The civic authorities had made arrangements with the owners of the Royal Hotel in Edinburgh to put the Newfoundlanders up free of cost during their stay. The First Battalion had spent their money freely while they were garrisoning Edinburgh Castle, and the authorities had not forgotten it.

I hated to leave those men of the First Battalion, who welcomed me so heartily. I was glad at the thought of getting back to the States again; but it was strange to think that I was no longer a soldier, that my days of fighting were over. An inexpressible sadness came over me as I bade good-by to them. Some of their names I do not know, but they were all my friends. There are others like them in various hospitals in England and Egypt; and also in a shady, tree-dotted ravine on the Peninsula of Gallipoli there is a row of graves, where also are my friends of the First Newfoundland Regiment.

The men our regiment lost, although they gladly fought a hopeless fight, have not died in vain. Constantinople has not been taken, and the Gallipoli campaign is fast becoming a memory, but things our men did there will not soon be forgotten. The foremost advance on the Suvla Bay front is Donnelly's Post on Caribou Ridge, made by the Newfoundlanders. It is called Donnelly's Post because it is here that Lieutenant Donnelly won his Military Cross. The hitherto unknown ridge from which the Turkish machine guns poured their concentrated death into our trenches stands as a monument to the initiative of the Newfoundlanders.

It is now Caribou Ridge as a recognition of the men who wear the deer's head badge. From Caribou Ridge the Turks could enfilade parts of our firing line. For weeks they had continued to pick off our men one by one. You could almost tell when your turn was coming. I know, because from Caribou Ridge came the bullet that sent me off the Peninsula. The machine guns on Caribou Ridge not only swept part of our trench, but commanded all of the intervening ground. This ground was almost absolutely devoid of cover. Several attempts had been made to rush those guns. All these attacks had failed, held up by the murderous machine-gun fire. Whole companies had essayed the task, but all had been repulsed, and almost annihilated. It remained for Lieutenant Donnelly to essay the impossible. Under cover of darkness, Lieutenant Donnelly, with only eight men, surprised the Turks in the post that now bears his name. The captured machine gun he turned on the Turks to repulse constantly launched bomb and rifle attacks. Just at dusk one evening Donnelly stole out to Caribou Ridge and took the Turks by storm. They had been accustomed before that to see large bodies of men swarm over the parapet in broad daylight, and had been able to wipe them out with machine-gun fire. All that night the Turks strove to recover their lost ground. The darkness that confused the enemy was the Newfoundlanders' ally. One of Donnelly's men, Jack Hynes, crawled away from his companions to a point about two hundred yards to the left. All through the night he poured a rapid stream of fire into the flank of the enemy's attacking party. So steadily did he keep it up that the Turks were deluded into thinking we had men there in force. When reinforcements arrived, Donnelly's eight men were reduced to two. Dawn showed the havoc wrought by the gallant little group. The ground in front of the post was a shambles of piled up Turkish corpses. But daylight showed something more to the credit of the Newfoundlanders than the mere taking of the ridge. It showed Jack Hynes purposely falling back over exposed ground to draw the enemy's attention from Sergeant Greene, who was coolly making trip after trip between the ridge and our lines, carrying a wounded man in his arms every time until all our wounded were in safety. Hynes and Greene were each given a Distinguished Conduct Medal. None was ever more nobly earned.

The night the First Newfoundland Regiment landed in Suvla Bay there were about eleven hundred of us. In December when the British forces evacuated Gallipoli, to our regiment fell the honour of being nominated to fight the rearguard action. This is the highest recognition a regiment can receive; for the duty of a rear guard in a retreat is to keep the enemy from reaching the main body of troops, even if this means annihilation for itself. At Lemnos Island the next day when the roll was called, of the eleven hundred men who landed when I did, only one hundred and seventy-one answered "Here."

After the First Newfoundland Regiment left the Peninsula, they went to Egypt to guard the Suez Canal from the long-expected attack of the Turks. After they had been rested a little while, they were recruited up to full fighting strength, again, and were sent to France. In the recent drive of the Allies against the German positions on the Somme, the regiment has won for itself fresh laurels. The *Times* correspondent at British headquarters in France sent the following on July 13th:

> The Newfoundlanders were the only overseas troops engaged in these operations. The story of their heroic part cannot yet be told in full, but when it is it will make Newfoundland very proud. The battalion was pushed up as what may be called the third wave in the attack on probably the most formidable section of the whole German front through an almost overwhelming artillery fire and a cross-ground swept by an enfilading machine-gun fire from hidden positions. The men behaved with completely noble steadiness and courage.

LEONAUR

ALSO FROM LEONAUR
AVAILABLE IN SOFTCOVER OR HARDCOVER WITH DUST JACKET

JOURNALS OF ROBERT ROGERS OF THE RANGERS *by Robert Rogers*—The exploits of Rogers & the Rangers in his own words during 1755-1761 in the French & Indian War.

GALLOPING GUNS *by James Young*—The Experiences of an Officer of the Bengal Horse Artillery During the Second Maratha War 1804-1805.

GORDON *by Demetrius Charles Boulger*—The Career of Gordon of Khartoum.

THE BATTLE OF NEW ORLEANS *by Zachary F. Smith*—The final major engagement of the War of 1812.

THE TWO WARS OF MRS DUBERLY *by Frances Isabella Duberly*—An Intrepid Victorian Lady's Experience of the Crimea and Indian Mutiny.

WITH THE GUARDS' BRIGADE DURING THE BOER WAR *by Edward P. Lowry*—On Campaign from Bloemfontein to Koomati Poort and Back.

THE REBELLIOUS DUCHESS *by Paul F. S. Dermoncourt*—The Adventures of the Duchess of Berri and Her Attempt to Overthrow French Monarchy.

MEN OF THE MUTINY *by John Tulloch Nash & Henry Metcalfe*—Two Accounts of the Great Indian Mutiny of 1857: Fighting with the Bengal Yeomanry Cavalry & Private Metcalfe at Lucknow.

CAMPAIGN IN THE CRIMEA *by George Shuldham Peard*—The Recollections of an Officer of the 20th Regiment of Foot.

WITHIN SEBASTOPOL *by K. Hodasevich*—A Narrative of the Campaign in the Crimea, and of the Events of the Siege.

WITH THE CAVALRY TO AFGHANISTAN *by William Taylor*—The Experiences of a Trooper of H. M. 4th Light Dragoons During the First Afghan War.

THE CAWNPORE MAN *by Mowbray Thompson*—A First Hand Account of the Siege and Massacre During the Indian Mutiny By One of Four Survivors.

BRIGADE COMMANDER: AFGHANISTAN *by Henry Brooke*—The Journal of the Commander of the 2nd Infantry Brigade, Kandahar Field Force During the Second Afghan War.

BANCROFT OF THE BENGAL HORSE ARTILLERY *by N. W. Bancroft*—An Account of the First Sikh War 1845-1846.

LEONAUR

ALSO FROM LEONAUR

AVAILABLE IN SOFTCOVER OR HARDCOVER WITH DUST JACKET

AFGHANISTAN: THE BELEAGUERED BRIGADE *by G. R. Gleig*—An Account of Sale's Brigade During the First Afghan War.

IN THE RANKS OF THE C. I. V *by Erskine Childers*—With the City Imperial Volunteer Battery (Honourable Artillery Company) in the Second Boer War.

THE BENGAL NATIVE ARMY *by F. G. Cardew*—An Invaluable Reference Resource.

THE 7TH (QUEEN'S OWN) HUSSARS: Volume 4—1688-1914 *by C. R. B. Barrett*—Uniforms, Equipment, Weapons, Traditions, the Services of Notable Officers and Men & the Appendices to All Volumes—Volume 4: 1688-1914.

THE SWORD OF THE CROWN *by Eric W. Sheppard*—A History of the British Army to 1914.

THE 7TH (QUEEN'S OWN) HUSSARS: Volume 3—1818-1914 *by C. R. B. Barrett*—On Campaign During the Canadian Rebellion, the Indian Mutiny, the Sudan, Matabeleland, Mashonaland and the Boer War Volume 3: 1818-1914.

THE KHARTOUM CAMPAIGN *by Bennet Burleigh*—A Special Correspondent's View of the Reconquest of the Sudan by British and Egyptian Forces under Kitchener—1898.

EL PUCHERO *by Richard McSherry*—The Letters of a Surgeon of Volunteers During Scott's Campaign of the American-Mexican War 1847-1848.

RIFLEMAN SAHIB *by E. Maude*—The Recollections of an Officer of the Bombay Rifles During the Southern Mahratta Campaign, Second Sikh War, Persian Campaign and Indian Mutiny.

THE KING'S HUSSAR *by Edwin Mole*—The Recollections of a 14th (King's) Hussar During the Victorian Era.

JOHN COMPANY'S CAVALRYMAN *by William Johnson*—The Experiences of a British Soldier in the Crimea, the Persian Campaign and the Indian Mutiny.

COLENSO & DURNFORD'S ZULU WAR *by Frances E. Colenso & Edward Durnford*—The first and possibly the most important history of the Zulu War.

U. S. DRAGOON *by Samuel E. Chamberlain*—Experiences in the Mexican War 1846-48 and on the South Western Frontier.

LEONAUR

ALSO FROM LEONAUR
AVAILABLE IN SOFTCOVER OR HARDCOVER WITH DUST JACKET

THE 2ND MAORI WAR: 1860-1861 *by Robert Carey*—The Second Maori War, or First Taranaki War, one more bloody instalment of the conflicts between European settlers and the indigenous Maori people.

A JOURNAL OF THE SECOND SIKH WAR *by Daniel A. Sandford*—The Experiences of an Ensign of the 2nd Bengal European Regiment During the Campaign in the Punjab, India, 1848-49.

THE LIGHT INFANTRY OFFICER *by John H. Cooke*—The Experiences of an Officer of the 43rd Light Infantry in America During the War of 1812.

BUSHVELDT CARBINEERS *by George Witton*—The War Against the Boers in South Africa and the 'Breaker' Morant Incident.

LAKE'S CAMPAIGNS IN INDIA *by Hugh Pearse*—The Second Anglo Maratha War, 1803-1807.

BRITAIN IN AFGHANISTAN 1: THE FIRST AFGHAN WAR 1839-42 *by Archibald Forbes*—From invasion to destruction-a British military disaster.

BRITAIN IN AFGHANISTAN 2: THE SECOND AFGHAN WAR 1878-80 *by Archibald Forbes*—This is the history of the Second Afghan War-another episode of British military history typified by savagery, massacre, siege and battles.

UP AMONG THE PANDIES *by Vivian Dering Majendie*—Experiences of a British Officer on Campaign During the Indian Mutiny, 1857-1858.

MUTINY: 1857 *by James Humphries*—Authentic Voices from the Indian Mutiny-First Hand Accounts of Battles, Sieges and Personal Hardships.

BLOW THE BUGLE, DRAW THE SWORD *by W. H. G. Kingston*—The Wars, Campaigns, Regiments and Soldiers of the British & Indian Armies During the Victorian Era, 1839-1898.

WAR BEYOND THE DRAGON PAGODA *by Major J. J. Snodgrass*—A Personal Narrative of the First Anglo-Burmese War 1824 - 1826.

THE HERO OF ALIWAL *by James Humphries*—The Campaigns of Sir Harry Smith in India, 1843-1846, During the Gwalior War & the First Sikh War.

ALL FOR A SHILLING A DAY *by Donald F. Featherstone*—The story of H.M. 16th, the Queen's Lancers During the first Sikh War 1845-1846.

LEONAUR

ALSO FROM LEONAUR
AVAILABLE IN SOFTCOVER OR HARDCOVER WITH DUST JACKET

OFFICERS & GENTLEMEN *by Peter Hawker & William Graham*—Two Accounts of British Officers During the Peninsula War: Officer of Light Dragoons by Peter Hawker & Campaign in Portugal and Spain by William Graham .

THE WALCHEREN EXPEDITION *by Anonymous*—The Experiences of a British Officer of the 81st Regt. During the Campaign in the Low Countries of 1809.

LADIES OF WATERLOO *by Charlotte A. Eaton, Magdalene de Lancey & Juana Smith*—The Experiences of Three Women During the Campaign of 1815: Waterloo Days by Charlotte A. Eaton, A Week at Waterloo by Magdalene de Lancey & Juana's Story by Juana Smith.

JOURNAL OF AN OFFICER IN THE KING'S GERMAN LEGION *by John Frederick Hering*—Recollections of Campaigning During the Napoleonic Wars.

JOURNAL OF AN ARMY SURGEON IN THE PENINSULAR WAR *by Charles Boutflower*—The Recollections of a British Army Medical Man on Campaign During the Napoleonic Wars.

ON CAMPAIGN WITH MOORE AND WELLINGTON *by Anthony Hamilton*—The Experiences of a Soldier of the 43rd Regiment During the Peninsular War.

THE ROAD TO AUSTERLITZ *by R. G. Burton*—Napoleon's Campaign of 1805.

SOLDIERS OF NAPOLEON *by A. J. Doisy De Villargennes & Arthur Chuquet*—The Experiences of the Men of the French First Empire: Under the Eagles by A. J. Doisy De Villargennes & Voices of 1812 by Arthur Chuquet .

INVASION OF FRANCE, 1814 *by F. W. O. Maycock*—The Final Battles of the Napoleonic First Empire.

LEIPZIG—A CONFLICT OF TITANS *by Frederic Shoberl*—A Personal Experience of the 'Battle of the Nations' During the Napoleonic Wars, October 14th-19th, 1813.

SLASHERS *by Charles Cadell*—The Campaigns of the 28th Regiment of Foot During the Napoleonic Wars by a Serving Officer.

BATTLE IMPERIAL *by Charles William Vane*—The Campaigns in Germany & France for the Defeat of Napoleon 1813-1814.

SWIFT & BOLD *by Gibbes Rigaud*—The 60th Rifles During the Peninsula War.

LEONAUR

ALSO FROM LEONAUR

AVAILABLE IN SOFTCOVER OR HARDCOVER WITH DUST JACKET

COLBORNE: A SINGULAR TALENT FOR WAR *by John Colborne*—The Napoleonic Wars Career of One of Wellington's Most Highly Valued Officers in Egypt, Holland, Italy, the Peninsula and at Waterloo.

NAPOLEON'S RUSSIAN CAMPAIGN *by Philippe Henri de Segur*—The Invasion, Battles and Retreat by an Aide-de-Camp on the Emperor's Staff.

WITH THE LIGHT DIVISION *by John H. Cooke*—The Experiences of an Officer of the 43rd Light Infantry in the Peninsula and South of France During the Napoleonic Wars.

WELLINGTON AND THE PYRENEES CAMPAIGN VOLUME I: FROM VITORIA TO THE BIDASSOA *by F. C. Beatson*—The final phase of the campaign in the Iberian Peninsula.

WELLINGTON AND THE INVASION OF FRANCE VOLUME II: THE BIDASSOA TO THE BATTLE OF THE NIVELLE *by F. C. Beatson*—The final phase of the campaign in the Iberian Peninsula.

WELLINGTON AND THE FALL OF FRANCE VOLUME III: THE GAVES AND THE BATTLE OF ORTHEZ *by F. C. Beatson*—The final phase of the campaign in the Iberian Peninsula.

NAPOLEON'S IMPERIAL GUARD: FROM MARENGO TO WATERLOO *by J. T. Headley*—The story of Napoleon's Imperial Guard and the men who commanded them.

BATTLES & SIEGES OF THE PENINSULAR WAR *by W. H. Fitchett*—Corunna, Busaco, Albuera, Ciudad Rodrigo, Badajos, Salamanca, San Sebastian & Others.

SERGEANT GUILLEMARD: THE MAN WHO SHOT NELSON? *by Robert Guillemard*—A Soldier of the Infantry of the French Army of Napoleon on Campaign Throughout Europe.

WITH THE GUARDS ACROSS THE PYRENEES *by Robert Batty*—The Experiences of a British Officer of Wellington's Army During the Battles for the Fall of Napoleonic France, 1813 .

A STAFF OFFICER IN THE PENINSULA *by E. W. Buckham*—An Officer of the British Staff Corps Cavalry During the Peninsula Campaign of the Napoleonic Wars.

THE LEIPZIG CAMPAIGN: 1813—NAPOLEON AND THE "BATTLE OF THE NATIONS" *by F. N. Maude*—Colonel Maude's analysis of Napoleon's campaign of 1813 around Leipzig.

ALSO FROM LEONAUR
AVAILABLE IN SOFTCOVER OR HARDCOVER WITH DUST JACKET

BUGEAUD: A PACK WITH A BATON by *Thomas Robert Bugeaud*—The Early Campaigns of a Soldier of Napoleon's Army Who Would Become a Marshal of France.

WATERLOO RECOLLECTIONS by *Frederick Llewellyn*—Rare First Hand Accounts, Letters, Reports and Retellings from the Campaign of 1815.

SERGEANT NICOL by *Daniel Nicol*—The Experiences of a Gordon Highlander During the Napoleonic Wars in Egypt, the Peninsula and France.

THE JENA CAMPAIGN: 1806 by *F. N. Maude*—The Twin Battles of Jena & Auerstadt Between Napoleon's French and the Prussian Army.

PRIVATE O'NEIL by *Charles O'Neil*—The recollections of an Irish Rogue of H. M. 28th Regt.—The Slashers—during the Peninsula & Waterloo campaigns of the Napoleonic war.

ROYAL HIGHLANDER by *James Anton*—A soldier of H.M 42nd (Royal) Highlanders during the Peninsular, South of France & Waterloo Campaigns of the Napoleonic Wars.

CAPTAIN BLAZE by *Elzéar Blaze*—Life in Napoleons Army.

LEJEUNE VOLUME 1 by *Louis-François Lejeune*—The Napoleonic Wars through the Experiences of an Officer on Berthier's Staff.

LEJEUNE VOLUME 2 by *Louis-François Lejeune*—The Napoleonic Wars through the Experiences of an Officer on Berthier's Staff.

CAPTAIN COIGNET by *Jean-Roch Coignet*—A Soldier of Napoleon's Imperial Guard from the Italian Campaign to Russia and Waterloo.

FUSILIER COOPER by *John S. Cooper*—Experiences in the 7th (Royal) Fusiliers During the Peninsular Campaign of the Napoleonic Wars and the American Campaign to New Orleans.

FIGHTING NAPOLEON'S EMPIRE by *Joseph Anderson*—The Campaigns of a British Infantryman in Italy, Egypt, the Peninsular & the West Indies During the Napoleonic Wars.

CHASSEUR BARRES by *Jean-Baptiste Barres*—The experiences of a French Infantryman of the Imperial Guard at Austerlitz, Jena, Eylau, Friedland, in the Peninsular, Lutzen, Bautzen, Zinnwald and Hanau during the Napoleonic Wars.

LEONAUR

ALSO FROM LEONAUR
AVAILABLE IN SOFTCOVER OR HARDCOVER WITH DUST JACKET

CAPTAIN COIGNET *by Jean-Roch Coignet*—A Soldier of Napoleon's Imperial Guard from the Italian Campaign to Russia and Waterloo.

HUSSAR ROCCA *by Albert Jean Michel de Rocca*—A French cavalry officer's experiences of the Napoleonic Wars and his views on the Peninsular Campaigns against the Spanish, British And Guerilla Armies.

MARINES TO 95TH (RIFLES) *by Thomas Fernyhough*—The military experiences of Robert Fernyhough during the Napoleonic Wars.

LIGHT BOB *by Robert Blakeney*—The experiences of a young officer in H.M 28th & 36th regiments of the British Infantry during the Peninsular Campaign of the Napoleonic Wars 1804 - 1814.

WITH WELLINGTON'S LIGHT CAVALRY *by William Tomkinson*—The Experiences of an officer of the 16th Light Dragoons in the Peninsular and Waterloo campaigns of the Napoleonic Wars.

SERGEANT BOURGOGNE *by Adrien Bourgogne*—With Napoleon's Imperial Guard in the Russian Campaign and on the Retreat from Moscow 1812 - 13.

SURTEES OF THE 95TH (RIFLES) *by William Surtees*—A Soldier of the 95th (Rifles) in the Peninsular campaign of the Napoleonic Wars.

SWORDS OF HONOUR *by Henry Newbolt & Stanley L. Wood*—The Careers of Six Outstanding Officers from the Napoleonic Wars, the Wars for India and the American Civil War.

ENSIGN BELL IN THE PENINSULAR WAR *by George Bell*—The Experiences of a young British Soldier of the 34th Regiment 'The Cumberland Gentlemen' in the Napoleonic wars.

HUSSAR IN WINTER *by Alexander Gordon*—A British Cavalry Officer during the retreat to Corunna in the Peninsular campaign of the Napoleonic Wars.

THE COMPLEAT RIFLEMAN HARRIS *by Benjamin Harris as told to and transcribed by Captain Henry Curling, 52nd Regt. of Foot*—The adventures of a soldier of the 95th (Rifles) during the Peninsular Campaign of the Napoleonic Wars.

THE ADVENTURES OF A LIGHT DRAGOON *by George Farmer & G.R. Gleig*—A cavalryman during the Peninsular & Waterloo Campaigns, in captivity & at the siege of Bhurtpore, India.

LEONAUR

ALSO FROM LEONAUR
AVAILABLE IN SOFTCOVER OR HARDCOVER WITH DUST JACKET

THE LIFE OF THE REAL BRIGADIER GERARD VOLUME 1—THE YOUNG HUSSAR 1782-1807 *by Jean-Baptiste De Marbot*—A French Cavalryman Of the Napoleonic Wars at Marengo, Austerlitz, Jena, Eylau & Friedland.

THE LIFE OF THE REAL BRIGADIER GERARD VOLUME 2—IMPERIAL AIDE-DE-CAMP 1807-1811 *by Jean-Baptiste De Marbot*—A French Cavalryman of the Napoleonic Wars at Saragossa, Landshut, Eckmuhl, Ratisbon, Aspern-Essling, Wagram, Busaco & Torres Vedras.

THE LIFE OF THE REAL BRIGADIER GERARD VOLUME 3—COLONEL OF CHASSEURS 1811-1815 *by Jean-Baptiste De Marbot*—A French Cavalryman in the retreat from Moscow, Lutzen, Bautzen, Katzbach, Leipzig, Hanau & Waterloo.

THE INDIAN WAR OF 1864 *by Eugene Ware*—The Experiences of a Young Officer of the 7th Iowa Cavalry on the Western Frontier During the Civil War.

THE MARCH OF DESTINY *by Charles E. Young & V. Devinny*—Dangers of the Trail in 1865 by Charles E. Young & The Story of a Pioneer by V. Devinny, two Accounts of Early Emigrants to Colorado.

CROSSING THE PLAINS *by William Audley Maxwell*—A First Hand Narrative of the Early Pioneer Trail to California in 1857.

CHIEF OF SCOUTS *by William F. Drannan*—A Pilot to Emigrant and Government Trains, Across the Plains of the Western Frontier.

THIRTY-ONE YEARS ON THE PLAINS AND IN THE MOUNTAINS *by William F. Drannan*—William Drannan was born to be a pioneer, hunter, trapper and wagon train guide during the momentous days of the Great American West.

THE INDIAN WARS VOLUNTEER *by William Thompson*—Recollections of the Conflict Against the Snakes, Shoshone, Bannocks, Modocs and Other Native Tribes of the American North West.

THE 4TH TENNESSEE CAVALRY *by George B. Guild*—The Services of Smith's Regiment of Confederate Cavalry by One of its Officers.

COLONEL WORTHINGTON'S SHILOH *by T. Worthington*—The Tennessee Campaign, 1862, by an Officer of the Ohio Volunteers.

FOUR YEARS IN THE SADDLE *by W. L. Curry*—The History of the First Regiment Ohio Volunteer Cavalry in the American Civil War.

LEONAUR

ALSO FROM LEONAUR

AVAILABLE IN SOFTCOVER OR HARDCOVER WITH DUST JACKET

LIFE IN THE ARMY OF NORTHERN VIRGINIA *by Carlton McCarthy*—The Observations of a Confederate Artilleryman of Cutshaw's Battalion During the American Civil War 1861-1865.

HISTORY OF THE CAVALRY OF THE ARMY OF THE POTOMAC *by Charles D. Rhodes*—Including Pope's Army of Virginia and the Cavalry Operations in West Virginia During the American Civil War.

CAMP-FIRE AND COTTON-FIELD *by Thomas W. Knox*—A New York Herald Correspondent's View of the American Civil War.

SERGEANT STILLWELL *by Leander Stillwell* —The Experiences of a Union Army Soldier of the 61st Illinois Infantry During the American Civil War.

STONEWALL'S CANNONEER *by Edward A. Moore*—Experiences with the Rockbridge Artillery, Confederate Army of Northern Virginia, During the American Civil War.

THE SIXTH CORPS *by George Stevens*—The Army of the Potomac, Union Army, During the American Civil War.

THE RAILROAD RAIDERS *by William Pittenger*—An Ohio Volunteers Recollections of the Andrews Raid to Disrupt the Confederate Railroad in Georgia During the American Civil War.

CITIZEN SOLDIER *by John Beatty*—An Account of the American Civil War by a Union Infantry Officer of Ohio Volunteers Who Became a Brigadier General.

COX: PERSONAL RECOLLECTIONS OF THE CIVIL WAR--VOLUME 1 *by Jacob Dolson Cox*—West Virginia, Kanawha Valley, Gauley Bridge, Cotton Mountain, South Mountain, Antietam, the Morgan Raid & the East Tennessee Campaign.

COX: PERSONAL RECOLLECTIONS OF THE CIVIL WAR--VOLUME 2 *by Jacob Dolson Cox*—Siege of Knoxville, East Tennessee, Atlanta Campaign, the Nashville Campaign & the North Carolina Campaign.

KERSHAW'S BRIGADE VOLUME 1 *by D. Augustus Dickert*—Manassas, Seven Pines, Sharpsburg (Antietam), Fredricksburg, Chancellorsville, Gettysburg, Chickamauga, Chattanooga, Fort Sanders & Bean Station.

KERSHAW'S BRIGADE VOLUME 2 *by D. Augustus Dickert*—At the wilderness, Cold Harbour, Petersburg, The Shenandoah Valley and Cedar Creek..

LEONAUR

ALSO FROM LEONAUR
AVAILABLE IN SOFTCOVER OR HARDCOVER WITH DUST JACKET

THE RELUCTANT REBEL by William G. Stevenson—A young Kentuckian's experiences in the Confederate Infantry & Cavalry during the American Civil War..

BOOTS AND SADDLES by Elizabeth B. Custer—The experiences of General Custer's Wife on the Western Plains.

FANNIE BEERS' CIVIL WAR by Fannie A. Beers—A Confederate Lady's Experiences of Nursing During the Campaigns & Battles of the American Civil War.

LADY SALE'S AFGHANISTAN by Florentia Sale—An Indomitable Victorian Lady's Account of the Retreat from Kabul During the First Afghan War.

THE TWO WARS OF MRS DUBERLY by Frances Isabella Duberly—An Intrepid Victorian Lady's Experience of the Crimea and Indian Mutiny.

THE REBELLIOUS DUCHESS by Paul F. S. Dermoncourt—The Adventures of the Duchess of Berri and Her Attempt to Overthrow French Monarchy.

LADIES OF WATERLOO by Charlotte A. Eaton, Magdalene de Lancey & Juana Smith—The Experiences of Three Women During the Campaign of 1815: Waterloo Days by Charlotte A. Eaton, A Week at Waterloo by Magdalene de Lancey & Juana's Story by Juana Smith.

TWO YEARS BEFORE THE MAST by Richard Henry Dana. Jr.—The account of one young man's experiences serving on board a sailing brig—the Penelope—bound for California, between the years1834-36.

A SAILOR OF KING GEORGE by Frederick Hoffman—From Midshipman to Captain—Recollections of War at Sea in the Napoleonic Age 1793-1815.

LORDS OF THE SEA by A. T. Mahan—Great Captains of the Royal Navy During the Age of Sail.

COGGESHALL'S VOYAGES: VOLUME 1 by George Coggeshall—The Recollections of an American Schooner Captain.

COGGESHALL'S VOYAGES: VOLUME 2 by George Coggeshall—The Recollections of an American Schooner Captain.

TWILIGHT OF EMPIRE by Sir Thomas Ussher & Sir George Cockburn—Two accounts of Napoleon's Journeys in Exile to Elba and St. Helena: Narrative of Events by Sir Thomas Ussher & Napoleon's Last Voyage: Extract of a diary by Sir George Cockburn.

LEONAUR

ALSO FROM LEONAUR
AVAILABLE IN SOFTCOVER OR HARDCOVER WITH DUST JACKET

ESCAPE FROM THE FRENCH by *Edward Boys*—A Young Royal Navy Midshipman's Adventures During the Napoleonic War.

THE VOYAGE OF H.M.S. PANDORA by *Edward Edwards R. N. & George Hamilton, edited by Basil Thomson*—In Pursuit of the Mutineers of the Bounty in the South Seas—1790-1791.

MEDUSA by *J. B. Henry Savigny and Alexander Correard and Charlotte-Adélaïde Dard* —Narrative of a Voyage to Senegal in 1816 & The Sufferings of the Picard Family After the Shipwreck of the Medusa.

THE SEA WAR OF 1812 VOLUME 1 by *A. T. Mahan*—A History of the Maritime Conflict.

THE SEA WAR OF 1812 VOLUME 2 by *A. T. Mahan*—A History of the Maritime Conflict.

WETHERELL OF H. M. S. HUSSAR by *John Wetherell*—The Recollections of an Ordinary Seaman of the Royal Navy During the Napoleonic Wars.

THE NAVAL BRIGADE IN NATAL by *C. R. N. Burne*—With the Guns of H. M. S. Terrible & H. M. S. Tartar during the Boer War 1899-1900.

THE VOYAGE OF H. M. S. BOUNTY by *William Bligh*—The True Story of an 18th Century Voyage of Exploration and Mutiny.

SHIPWRECK! by *William Gilly*—The Royal Navy's Disasters at Sea 1793-1849.

KING'S CUTTERS AND SMUGGLERS: 1700-1855 by *E. Keble Chatterton*—A unique period of maritime history-from the beginning of the eighteenth to the middle of the nineteenth century when British seamen risked all to smuggle valuable goods from wool to tea and spirits from and to the Continent.

CONFEDERATE BLOCKADE RUNNER by *John Wilkinson*—The Personal Recollections of an Officer of the Confederate Navy.

NAVAL BATTLES OF THE NAPOLEONIC WARS by *W. H. Fitchett*—Cape St.Vincent, the Nile, Cadiz, Copenhagen, Trafalgar & Others.

PRISONERS OF THE RED DESERT by *R. S. Gwatkin-Williams*—The Adventures of the Crew of the Tara During the First World War.

U-BOAT WAR 1914-1918 by *James B. Connolly/Karl von Schenk*—Two Contrasting Accounts from Both Sides of the Conflict at Sea D uring the Great War.

LEONAUR

ALSO FROM LEONAUR
AVAILABLE IN SOFTCOVER OR HARDCOVER WITH DUST JACKET

FARAWAY CAMPAIGN *by F. James*—Experiences of an Indian Army Cavalry Officer in Persia & Russia During the Great War.

REVOLT IN THE DESERT *by T. E. Lawrence*—An account of the experiences of one remarkable British officer's war from his own perspective.

MACHINE-GUN SQUADRON *by A. M. G.*—The 20th Machine Gunners from British Yeomanry Regiments in the Middle East Campaign of the First World War.

A GUNNER'S CRUSADE *by Antony Bluett*—The Campaign in the Desert, Palestine & Syria as Experienced by the Honourable Artillery Company During the Great War .

DESPATCH RIDER *by W. H. L. Watson*—The Experiences of a British Army Motorcycle Despatch Rider During the Opening Battles of the Great War in Europe.

TIGERS ALONG THE TIGRIS *by E. J. Thompson*—The Leicestershire Regiment in Mesopotamia During the First World War.

HEARTS & DRAGONS *by Charles R. M. F. Crutwell*—The 4th Royal Berkshire Regiment in France and Italy During the Great War, 1914-1918.

INFANTRY BRIGADE: 1914 *by John Ward*—The Diary of a Commander of the 15th Infantry Brigade, 5th Division, British Army, During the Retreat from Mons.

DOING OUR 'BIT' *by Ian Hay*—Two Classic Accounts of the Men of Kitchener's 'New Army' During the Great War including *The First 100,000* & *All In It*.

AN EYE IN THE STORM *by Arthur Ruhl*—An American War Correspondent's Experiences of the First World War from the Western Front to Gallipoli-and Beyond.

STAND & FALL *by Joe Cassells*—With the Middlesex Regiment Against the Bolsheviks 1918-19.

RIFLEMAN MACGILL'S WAR *by Patrick MacGill*—A Soldier of the London Irish During the Great War in Europe including *The Amateur Army*, *The Red Horizon* & *The Great Push*.

WITH THE GUNS *by C. A. Rose & Hugh Dalton*—Two First Hand Accounts of British Gunners at War in Europe During World War 1- Three Years in France with the Guns and With the British Guns in Italy.

THE BUSH WAR DOCTOR *by Robert V. Dolbey*—The Experiences of a British Army Doctor During the East African Campaign of the First World War.

LEONAUR

ALSO FROM LEONAUR
AVAILABLE IN SOFTCOVER OR HARDCOVER WITH DUST JACKET

THE 9TH—THE KING'S (LIVERPOOL REGIMENT) IN THE GREAT WAR 1914 - 1918 *by Enos H. G. Roberts*—Mersey to mud—war and Liverpool men.

THE GAMBARDIER *by Mark Severn*—The experiences of a battery of Heavy artillery on the Western Front during the First World War.

FROM MESSINES TO THIRD YPRES *by Thomas Floyd*—A personal account of the First World War on the Western front by a 2/5th Lancashire Fusilier.

THE IRISH GUARDS IN THE GREAT WAR - VOLUME 1 *by Rudyard Kipling*—Edited and Compiled from Their Diaries and Papers—The First Battalion.

THE IRISH GUARDS IN THE GREAT WAR - VOLUME 1 *by Rudyard Kipling*—Edited and Compiled from Their Diaries and Papers—The Second Battalion.

ARMOURED CARS IN EDEN *by K. Roosevelt*—An American President's son serving in Rolls Royce armoured cars with the British in Mesopatamia & with the American Artillery in France during the First World War.

CHASSEUR OF 1914 *by Marcel Dupont*—Experiences of the twilight of the French Light Cavalry by a young officer during the early battles of the great war in Europe.

TROOP HORSE & TRENCH *by R.A. Lloyd*—The experiences of a British Lifeguardsman of the household cavalry fighting on the western front during the First World War 1914-18.

THE EAST AFRICAN MOUNTED RIFLES *by C.J. Wilson*—Experiences of the campaign in the East African bush during the First World War.

THE LONG PATROL *by George Berrie*—A Novel of Light Horsemen from Gallipoli to the Palestine campaign of the First World War.

THE FIGHTING CAMELIERS *by Frank Reid*—The exploits of the Imperial Camel Corps in the desert and Palestine campaigns of the First World War.

STEEL CHARIOTS IN THE DESERT *by S. C. Rolls*—The first world war experiences of a Rolls Royce armoured car driver with the Duke of Westminster in Libya and in Arabia with T.E. Lawrence.

WITH THE IMPERIAL CAMEL CORPS IN THE GREAT WAR *by Geoffrey Inchbald*—The story of a serving officer with the British 2nd battalion against the Senussi and during the Palestine campaign.

www.ingramcontent.com/pod-product-compliance
Lightning Source LLC
Chambersburg PA
CBHW021005090426
42738CB00007B/662